Chronicles

of the
South Carolina
Sea Islands

D0969532

Carolina Seashells

Tales of the South Carolina Low Country

More Tales of the South Carolina Low Country

Coastal Ghosts: Haunted Places from Wilmington to Savannah

Once Upon a Time on a Plantation

Plantation Tales

Alice Flagg: The Ghost of the Hermitage

Touring the Coastal South Carolina Backroads

The South Carolina Lizard Man

Touring the Coastal Georgia Backroads

The Jack-O'-Lantern Ghost

Southern Recipes and Legends

John Henry Rutledge: The Ghost of Hampton Plantation (as if told by Sue Alston)

Chronicles

of the

South Carolina

Sea Islands

NANCY RHYNE

JOHN F. BLAIR, PUBLISHER
WINSTON-SALEM, NORTH CAROLINA

BOOK DESIGN BY DEBRA LONG HAMPTON
PHOTOGRAPHS BY SID RHYNE
PRINTED AND BOUND BY EDWARDS BROTHERS

*The paper in this book meets
the guidelines for permanence and durability
of the Committee on Production Guidelines
for Book Longevity of the
Council on Library Resources*

Photograph on front cover and page iii—
The area where Drunken Jack Island once stood

Library of Congress Cataloging-in-Publication Data

Rhyne, Nancy, 1926–
Chronicles of the South Carolina sea islands / Nancy Rhyne.
        p.   cm.
  Includes bibliographical references (p.   ) and index.
        ISBN 0-89587-208-0 (alk. paper)
1. Sea Islands—History—Anecdotes.   2. South Carolina—
        History—Anecdotes.   I. Title.
              F277.A19R47   1998
        975.7'99—dc21   97–40069

To

Wynness Thomas
and our writing conferences
at the Biscuit Shack

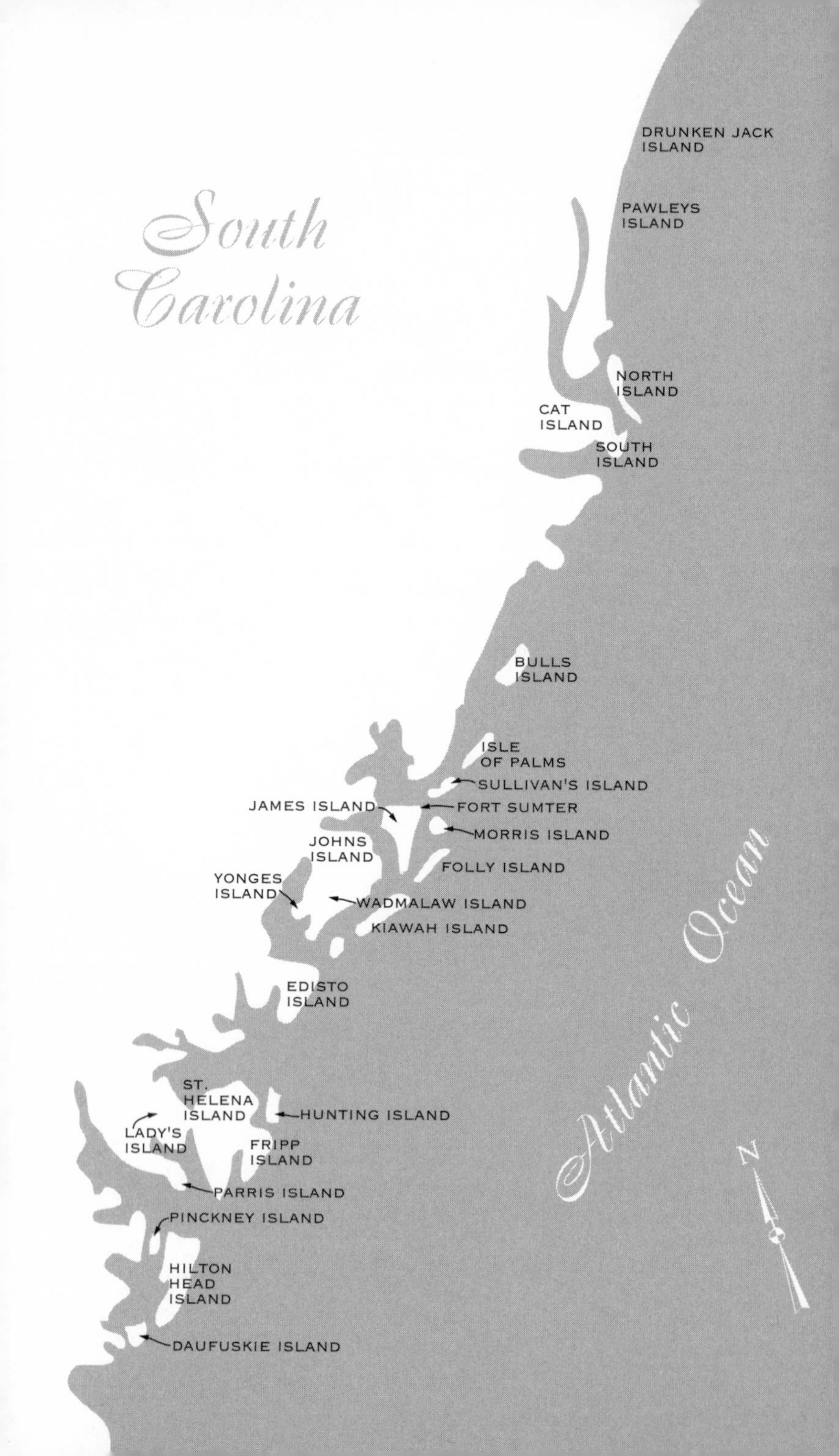

South Carolina

DRUNKEN JACK
ISLAND

PAWLEYS
ISLAND

NORTH
ISLAND

CAT
ISLAND

SOUTH
ISLAND

BULLS
ISLAND

ISLE
OF PALMS

SULLIVAN'S ISLAND

JAMES ISLAND

FORT SUMTER

MORRIS ISLAND

JOHNS
ISLAND

FOLLY ISLAND

YONGES
ISLAND

WADMALAW ISLAND

KIAWAH ISLAND

EDISTO
ISLAND

ST.
HELENA
ISLAND

HUNTING ISLAND

LADY'S
ISLAND

FRIPP
ISLAND

PARRIS ISLAND

PINCKNEY ISLAND

HILTON
HEAD
ISLAND

DAUFUSKIE ISLAND

Atlantic Ocean

N

Contents

Acknowledgments   ix
Introduction   1

Drunken Jack Island   7
Pawleys Island   13
North Island   21
South Island   28
Cat Island   34
Bulls Island   38
Isle of Palms   44
Sullivan's Island   48
Fort Sumter   54
James Island, Folly Island, and Morris Island   58
Johns Island   69
Wadmalaw Island   78
Kiawah Island   85
Yonges Island   92
Edisto Island   102
Lady's Island   124
St. Helena Island   129
Hunting Island   140
Fripp Island   144
Parris Island   148
Pinckney Island   154
Hilton Head Island   159
Daufuskie Island   172

Bibliography   181
Index   184

Acknowledgments

As always, I owe a special thanks to the staff of Chapin Memorial Library in Myrtle Beach: Cathy Wiggins, the library director, and Sharon White, the administrative secretary; Shirley Wayland, the assistant director; Mary Owens, Linda Maher, and Grace Kicidis in the Circulation Department; Lesta Sue Hardee and Ernestine Gates in the Technical Services Department; Sue Ellen Wilson and Lee Oates in the Children's Department; and Cindy Herrington and Linda Goff, reference assistants.

Kudos also go to the staff of the Caroliniana Library in Columbia, and especially to the students who made my many photocopies.

I owe thanks to Jack Little, director of Bonnie Doone Plantation in Walterboro, where I am on the Elderhostel faculty. Had Jack not asked me to teach a course entitled "Sea Island Odyssey," it is unlikely that I would have done the research on South Carolina's barrier islands necessary for this book.

As always, I am grateful to my husband, Sid, for making the photos, for always encouraging me, and for helping me with research and slides for the Bonnie Doone Plantation Elderhostel programs "Things That Go Bump" and "Sea Island Odyssey."

Strolling along the beach on Daufuskie Island

Rockville homes

Deer along the
roadside on
Hunting Island

Introduction

$\mathscr{S}outh$ $\mathscr{C}arolina's$ sea islands
begin just north of Georgetown and
continue south to the Georgia state
line. There are an estimated one thousand of these islands, separated from
the mainland by marshes and rivers.
They range in size from tiny, uninhab-
itable islets to islands large enough to
accommodate numerous sea-island
cotton plantations. Johns Island, just

south of Charleston, is the second-largest island in the United States.

From the earliest settlement by Europeans, the islands have proven themselves highly valuable agricultural lands. Indigo production was the first great breakthrough. And untold fortunes were made from the rice grown on plantations adjacent to the rivers emptying into the Atlantic. But the story of South Carolina's sea islands is really that of long-staple cotton. Throughout much of recorded history, the sea-island cotton grown here was considered the best in the world and brought its growers profits on an unimaginable scale. The stunning plantations built by the growers of sea-island cotton are the stuff of which romance novels are made. To fictionalize the lifestyle of the planters would be to sell short the true story that began with the seed.

It was 1736 when seed was obtained in the Bahamas. The first attempt to raise a crop in South Carolina was made in 1788 by Mrs. Kinsey Burden of Burden's Island, St. Paul's Parish. The first legitimate crop was raised on Hilton Head by William Elliott in 1790. The following year, John Screven planted thirty to forty acres in St. Luke's Parish. After that, the race was on.

It was found that the light, sandy soil of the coastal regions of South Carolina and Georgia was best suited for the production of this grade of cotton. Altogether, the sea-island cotton belt was a twenty- to thirty-mile-wide stretch of coastal land from the Santee River to the Everglades of Florida. The finest of all long-staple cotton was grown on the sea islands within a mile or two of the ocean. Cotton raised a few miles inland on the same island had a coarser fiber and did not command the highest price.

Though the profitability of cotton production was quickly obvious, an efficient method of separating the fibers from the seeds had to be found. An early roller gin squeezed the seeds from the fiber, but a much better method came in 1793 when Eli Whitney invented the sawtooth cotton gin at Mulberry Grove Plantation on the Savannah River.

The planters used salt-marsh mulch and oyster shells as fertilizer. The growing season lasted from March until September, when the bolls burst open. The cotton was painstakingly separated, dried, whipped, sorted, ginned, cleaned, and then packed into large, round loads and barged to its final destination—the agents in Charleston and Savannah, and thus the world market.

One skillful planter began taking special care in selecting seed. By noting his results year after year, he improved the staple. In 1825, he sold his crop at $1.16 per pound. Three years later, by virtue of his attention to selection and cultivation, he sold his cotton for $2.00 per pound. It was not long before other planters followed his lead.

The selection process required delicate hands. Indeed, so careful of their hands were these planters that they wore gloves. A few became so expert that they could pick up a wad of cotton, feel it, spin it into a thread with their fingers, and announce on which plantation it had been grown.

By the 1820s, South Carolina and Georgia were producing about half the total cotton crop in the United States. Sea-island cotton had a flower of a rich cream color and a fiber that sometimes reached two and a half inches in length. Since its fiber was so white, extra care had to be taken in production. This was the most tedious part of the process. In fact, it cost a planter an average of seventeen dollars to gin a 250-pound bale. One planter estimated that in the early days of production, fifty-four laborers were required to prepare seed cotton for market: a dryer, a turner, a feeder, thirty pickers, seven field levelers, twelve ginners, a packer, and an inspector.

Slaves were the force that drove cotton production. Planters stocked up on slaves at the Charleston market. In 1860, the average number of slaves per owner on the sea islands was 30, double that of the state of South Carolina as a whole. Twenty percent of the planters owned more than 50 slaves. Only one planter owned more than 500. The Beaufort area was one of the most thickly populated slave districts in the entire South. *Simms' Geography* gives the population of that district in 1840 as 35,894, of whom 29,682 were slaves.

The planters cultivated about six acres per slave and got an average yield of about 135 pounds per acre. As there were few plows, most of the cultivation was done with hoes. Provision crops were worked only when time could be spared from cotton. The usual result was that provisions were not sufficient to last the year and had to be bought.

On many sea-island plantations, the only white people were the planter families and the overseer. Thanks to the islands' isolation and the large proportion of slaves, the effect of white culture on the slave population was minimal. The tendency for a distinct black culture to emerge was thus stronger on the islands than in other slave areas.

The slaves on South Carolina's sea islands spoke a language known as Gullah. According to Dr. Charles Joyner, an authority on Gullah speech, the language formed plurals and indicated possession and negation differently from English. It used a simpler system of pronouns and a more complex system of verbs. There was no distinction between male and female pronouns, the all-purpose form being 'e: "After de war, 'e come back and Maussa pay 'em wages." A form of Gullah is still spoken on some sea islands, but it has been vastly corrupted from the original language.

The planters built spectacular homes of tabby, brick, or wood in Charleston, Beaufort, and Savannah. These houses had several stories, thick walls, recessed windows, and white columns supporting spacious piazzas. The interiors were beautifully wainscoted and paneled. They had hand-carved moldings and cornices, mantels of fine wood or imported marble, and curving mahogany stairs. The furniture came from Europe. The portraits were painted by Thomas Sully, Charleston portraitist. The planters sent their sons to England for their education before the Revolutionary War and to Princeton, Harvard, Yale, and South Carolina College in Charleston after it.

The cultivation of sea-island cotton suffered setbacks during and after the Civil War. Indeed, so scarce was seed that it was said all the long-staple cotton grown subsequently arose from the seed that a single planter had saved in an envelope. Sea-island cotton had other enemies as well: weeds, Bermuda grass, blight, grasshoppers. But the death knell was not sounded until the arrival of the boll weevil in 1919. Due to its early maturity, short-staple cotton could still be raised in spite of the weevil, but the sea-island grade did not mature until much later, usually in October, thus giving the weevil more time to consume it. Practically no long-staple cotton has been grown in South Carolina since 1920.

From about the turn of the twentieth century until World

War II, many of South Carolina's sea islands were bought by wealthy Northerners for use as hunting preserves. The hunting escapades on these islands have never been fully chronicled, but brief histories exist for some of the larger islands. Descendants of the original Northern sportsmen still own some islands.

Gone are the days of sea-island territorial units, fields facing the sea, long-staple cotton piled high on wagons, and white-gloved masters examining their product to determine its quality. Gone, too, are many of the great mansions. The sea-island cotton plantations were destined to fade into the pages of history.

Today, some of the islands are state parks or nature preserves. Others are resort areas with dream houses constructed by top-flight architects. Others remain in their wild state. Others no longer exist.

The pages that follow reflect on South Carolina's sea islands, from Drunken Jack in the north to Daufuskie in the south. With one or two exceptions, I have limited my coverage to those islands that visitors can actually explore for themselves. I eliminated from consideration those numerous islands that are exceedingly small, inaccessible, or private. I have addressed the principal islands individually, recounting historical events and tales.

Should you travel the coast and visit these islands, you will likely enjoy an experience that will surpass your expectations. If you cannot journey to them, may you be in the company of the planter families as you travel the chapters of this book with me.

DRUNKEN JACK ISLAND

The area where Drunken Jack Island once stood

It may seem curious to begin this book with an island that cannot be visited anymore—indeed, an island that exists only at low tide, and barely then. But in a way, Drunken Jack Island typifies South Carolina's sea islands in its isolation; in its lush, exotic vegetation; in its legends from pre–Revolutionary War days; in its wealth and glory in the years before the Civil War; and, most important, in its ultimate fragility in the face of the mighty ocean.

South of Myrtle Beach at Murrells Inlet, near what is now Huntington Beach State Park, was a narrow, circuitous water route known as "the Mouth." Only pilots familiar with every sand bar and oyster reef could safely guide ships into the quiet waters of the inlet beyond "the Mouth." Just within the inlet was an island covered with scrubby live oaks, prickly pears, cedars half-buried by sand dunes, dwarf live oaks, myrtles, and an occasional lonesome pine. There were also tangled masses of morning glories and great growths of Spanish bayonet. Two meandering tidewater creeks on the island were prolific producers of oysters and clams.

In the days when Stede Bonnet, Captain Kidd, and other notorious buccaneers ravaged the South Carolina coast, it was this island that afforded a resting place to a pirate known only as Jacque. Little is known of Jacque other than that his love of drink was the cause of his undoing. After a prolonged spree left him in a weakened condition, he died here and was buried behind a sand dune by his crew. Honorable man or not, he was honored for centuries by the island's name: Drunken Jack.

Just after the Civil War, a group of men mysteriously appeared on the island. Guided by a chart, they located a certain tall pine nearly two feet in diameter and began to dig. They then vanished as quietly as they had come, leaving only the signs of their excavations. Whether on not they carried off Jacque's treasure chests is unknown, but the story of their visit was still being told as late as 1936 by the local schoolmaster, who had visited the site and seen queer notches cut into the pine when he was a boy.

Others say the island was named for Jack Green, a six-foot-four-inch, three-hundred-pound Revolutionary War veteran who was a member of the famous Hot and Hot Fish Club in the early years of the eighteenth century.

Drunken Jack Island was the site of the first club by that unusual name. In the days when rice cultivation bestowed great wealth on members of the planter class on this part of the coast, the planters created gun clubs and fish clubs to increase their enjoyment of their leisure time.

The stated purpose of the Hot and Hot Fish Club was the promotion of "convivial and social intercourse" over good food and wine. Rice planter J. Motte Alston (1821–1909) described the routine in his memoirs: "Each member brought his own dish or dishes, wines, etc. Each member brought his servant; and when all the good things had been discussed, interwoven with some politics and thrice told anecdotes . . . night began to throw her mantle over the happy members of the Hot and Hot Fish Club."

After the planters arrived with their covered dishes, a young fisherman would be sent out into the ocean to bring back a catch. As soon as he returned with his boatload of fish, it was cooked and served hot. Meanwhile, he was sent out for a second boatload, which was cooked and served hot as a second helping. The club's name thus recognized the two separate servings.

Annual membership dues eventually reached fifty dollars per person, a considerable sum for anyone except aristocrats in those days. The club's bylaw XIV sheds light on the nature of the membership. It read, "Any member of this Club, who shall be elected or appointed to any distinguished office in this State, shall for each and every such compliment, furnish for the use of the Club one box of champagne." This was no idle rule, as the members included one South Carolina governor, two lieutenant governors, and twenty-one planter-politicians who went by the title of "Esquire," not to mention one general, eleven colonels, two majors, two captains, and ten doctors.

The club boasted a tenpin alley, a billiard table, and a race-course. The facilities on Drunken Jack were the first of five in-carnations of the Hot and Hot Fish Club. The club was dis-mantled and laid finally to rest by former slaves after the Civil War.

Drunken Jack Island may be best remembered for the deadly hurricane that crashed there.

People on and around Drunken Jack began noticing ominous signs around sundown on October 12, 1893. The Reverend Cato Singleton was one of the first. "The tide ain't run out that day," he remembered. "Not even for to show ister rock [mounds of oyster shells], ner neither sand bar. That sea make us think of judgment and hell. He look like he on fire. The creek been light up. Sea and creek been shine."

Dr. Arthur Flagg, Sr., and many members of his extended fam-ily were staying in adjacent cottages on Drunken Jack with their servants. During the night, J. Ward Flagg heard someone in the hallway outside his room say, "I believe there has been an earth-quake at sea."

His mother's voice called out, "Put your faith in God. Go back to bed."

As daylight broke on Friday the thirteenth, the marsh was flood-ing on what was supposed to be a low tide. Everyone began to talk about the recent hurricane of August 27, when three thou-sand people south of Charleston had lost their lives.

By ten o'clock in the morning, the sky was black as midnight. A servant at a nearby cottage called at the Arthur Flagg, Sr., house and offered refuge at the cottage where she worked. The offer was turned down.

All at once, it got even blacker. J. Ward Flagg shouted, "Everybody, swim to the cedar tree!" Arthur Flagg, Sr., and one of his sons helped Mrs. Flagg and some children and servants out to the tree, which was still rooted.

Forty-foot waves crashed over the tree. When Arthur Flagg, Sr., saw his wife, Georgeanna, lose her grip, he let go of the tree and grabbed her. J. Ward Flagg caught them and pulled them back, but he could not hold them for long before they went to sea. The entire cottage they had fled was gone by then. The wind grew so fierce that the clothes were ripped from the bodies of those holding the tree. Elizabeth and Pauline Weston, nieces of J. Ward Flagg, lost their hold and were engulfed by the water.

By eleven-thirty, the worst of the storm was over, and the sun came out. By afternoon, stories began to trickle out of Drunken Jack. Not only had several members of the Arthur Flagg, Sr., household lost their lives, but everyone in the adjacent cottage—inhabited by Arthur Flagg, Jr., and his family—was dead. So many bodies were taken to All Saints Episcopal Church to await burial that the overflow of pine boxes was put by the side of the road.

Eyewitnesses remembered the storm as long as they lived.

"The whole county was in mourning," wrote Flora McDonald LaBruce.

"I remember too good that storm," recalled one woman. "We had a loft. Got up there. Leak? Rained through like outdoors."

"The beach was gone," said Ben Horry. "After the ocean went back, bodies were as thick as marsh grass. But some washed out to the Gulf Stream."

"The moss flew from tree same like bird," said the Reverend Cato Singleton. "The wind talked and moaned same like human.

And every which way trees snapped. People went down in prayer. Called on the Lord to carry us through. Asked God to speak to the wind and waves. Asked Him to calm the elements. . . . And God called them back. The waves obeyed. Rolled out. Rolled back to the deep. Much corpse lay in the marsh. A cow hung in live oak tree. Carcass hung high. The buzzard feasted."

"The date of my birth?" asked Mariah Heywood. "How would I know? It went to sea in Dr. Flagg's Bible."

For years, the hurricane was known locally as "the Flagg Storm," since it wiped out most of that family.

Today, nothing remains of Drunken Jack Island save some clam banks and oyster reefs covered at high tide. However, one can visit Huntington Beach State Park and see the area where Drunken Jack once stood. In fact, the park's huge, moss-draped live oaks, uncrowded beach, and sand dunes covered in sea oats are the exact landscape once enjoyed by the privileged members of the Hot and Hot Fish Club.

The Pawley House

Pawleys Island was named for Percival Pawley, whose will listed among his many holdings "one great Ile." Pawley was a mariner who lived in what is now Berkeley County. He held land grants as early as 1711, one of them for the territory from the "Waccamau River to the sea marsh." He willed his land to his children.

George Pawley, the most prominent of Percival's sons, was a member of the local assembly. He also served as commissioner of the pilotage, commissioner of Lynch's Causeway, commissioner of the parish church of Prince George, and commissioner of the roads on Waccamaw Neck.

Less than four miles in length and a quarter-mile wide at its widest point, Pawleys Island has been featured in the *New York Times* and several travel magazines. As beach resorts go, it's a breath of fresh air. How did this rather isolated island, where there are no fast-food restaurants or high-rise hotels, achieve vacation stardom? The answer is quite simple: because of people's passion for a beach resort in its natural purity.

It all started with the wealthy rice planters.

In the late 1790s, the planter families were terrorized by what they called "summer fever"—malarial fever. It would be years before anyone knew the culprit was the anopheles mosquito, which bred in the low-lying rice fields.

In order to get away from the fever, some planters moved their families to the "Up Country" and others built houses on the sea islands. Families with summer homes at Pawleys traveled to the island by boat until the causeway was built in 1846. The causeway was constructed by future South Carolina governor Robert Francis Withers Allston using about fifty slaves with wagons and mule teams.

Beach houses at Pawleys were constructed of cypress, called "the everlasting wood." That claim is justified: ten of the original houses on the island remain to this day, witnesses to untold hurricanes. The longevity of the old Pawleys houses is also thanks in part to the practice of building them behind dunes or on stilts.

The gaps between the aged floorboards have helped, too. Water can enter and drain from an old house more easily than from a new, tight house, which is likelier to be pushed off its foundation. The sloping porches of the old homes were built to allow runoff.

Pieces of framework with mortise and tenon joints were prepared on the plantations. After Roman numerals were chiseled on each piece, the lumber was floated down to the island. Slave carpenters assembled the houses by matching the multidigit Roman numerals. At least one of the slaves, Renty, a master carpenter at Hagley Plantation, had been sent to England to learn his trade. It is amazing how well the pieces fit after being floated miles to the island.

The servants' houses had two rooms and a chimney. Additional outbuildings on the property were the kitchen, the chicken house, the stable, and the "necessary."

The planters didn't blink an eye at shipping furniture and other items to the beach for the summer months. Sometimes, a piano was taken so the daughters of the family could practice their music. Horses were transported for early-morning rides on the beach. Books were taken in order to have reading material at hand, and some account books were worked on by the plantation masters.

Unlike the great plantation manor houses and Charleston mansions, the planters' houses on Pawleys were plain. No one took pains to see that the china and silver were a match, and there were few ornaments. Any embellishment usually consisted of seashells or native greenery.

The original houses can be recognized by their wraparound

porches, their dormer windows, and the brick pillars that raise them high off the ground. Some of these pillars were constructed of bricks used as ballast in ships traveling from England to America. Each old beach house has a historical marker near the driveway.

One of these structures is the Plowden Weston residence, known today as The Pelican Inn. Plowden Weston was the lieutenant governor of South Carolina from 1862 to 1864. He obtained his Pawleys land in 1844.

The summer residence of Robert Francis Withers Allston (1801–64) also stands today. At the end of each May, the entire Allston household migrated to the sea. Though Pawleys Island was just four miles east of the family plantation, reaching it required a journey of seven miles by boat and four more by land. Vehicles, horses, cows, furniture, bedding, trunks, and piano were sent ahead. The family traveled in rowboats as oarsmen sang old-time spirituals, keeping tempo with the pulling of the oars.

Elizabeth Allston Pringle, daughter of Robert Francis Withers Allston, described her island summers in her book *Chronicles of Chicora Wood*:

> We went to our summer home on Pawley's in June, and oh! the delight of the freedom of the life on the sea-beach after the city, and the happiness of being at home. The bathing in the glorious surf early in the morning—we often saw the sun rise while we were in the water, for we were a very early household, and had breakfast at what would now be thought an unearthly hour, but my father did a tremendous day's work, which could only be accomplished by rising before the sun.

The Pelican Inn

And we children were by no means idle. We were required to read and write and practise every day. Papa's rules were strict: we could never go out to walk or play on the beach in the afternoon unless we had done our tasks. I was required to practise only half an hour, but it must be done. Then I wrote a page in a blank book and showed it to mamma for correction. She had me to write a journal of all that had taken place the day before, instead of writing in my copy-book. . . . Add to this that papa did not allow us to read a story-book or a novel before the three-o'clock dinner, so that I read by myself in the mornings Motley's *Rise of the Dutch Republic* and Prescott's *Philip II* only a little portion every day, but there is no telling how much my taste was formed by it.

Besides the Allston House and The Pelican Inn, the original houses still standing are Casamar, Sandy Cot, the Pawley House, All Saints Summer Parsonage, Liberty Lodge, the LaBruce-Lemon House, the Nesbit-Noburn House, and the Summer Academy, which was rebuilt after Hurricane Hugo nearly demolished it. These houses are among the oldest summer residences in continuous use in the United States.

It was well into the twentieth century before electricity and running water reached the island. By 1919, house parties at Pawleys were common—and invitations envied. Vacationers arrived at the old houses by automobile. Ladies' bathing attire consisted of below-the-knee dresses; most women wore bathing caps when they ventured into the surf. Men wore knee-length britches and sleeveless shirts. Bathing shoes were worn by all. Sports in-

The kitchen of the LaBruce-Lemon House

cluded crabbing, shrimping, surf bathing, surf fishing, duck hunting, and deer driving.

Pawleys Island crab cakes and sturgeon are legendary. During the 1930s, the son of a Pawleys Island cook talked about the sturgeon served on the island: "Now, sturgeon a valuable fish. Valuablest fish you find in water. Sturgeon fish bring seventy-five cents a pound. Sturgeon egg cost you a dollar a pound, wholesale. Catcher get a dollar a pound. Me and Cap'n Lachicotte catch one had in him twenty-five pounds of roe. Cost twenty-five dollars for roe, fifteen dollars for fish. Cut the head off. Cut off the tail. Cut off the fin. Sell him dressed."

By the 1940s, Pawleys Island had become established as a choice vacation spot. Rental agencies were thriving. Dancing the Big Apple was the island passion. For college students, Easter house parties were the event of the year. The most complicated decisions involved whether to loll in a Pawleys Island hammock and read a novel or take a crab net to the creek.

During recent years, many homes have been built on Pawleys, most of them in a style compatible with the original beach houses. A road extends the length of the island. On a part of the road running between the ocean and the creek, one can view the owners' piers jutting into the creek. Isolated and private, Pawleys remains much the same today as it has been for well over a century.

No discussion of Pawleys is complete without a mention of the island's most famous visitor. The legendary Gray Man is a ghost that appears on the beach before hurricanes. He says nothing, but by virtue of seeing him, a person is guaranteed safety. The Gray Man was seen as early as 1800 and as recently as September

1989, just before Hurricane Hugo. Those who have seen him claim they were filled with a sense of contentment and safety, even though they knew a deadly storm was imminent. They further claim that their property was saved by the Gray Man, though other properties were washed away during the storm.

Should you be walking on the sand at Pawleys Island and see a man in gray, don't pass it off lightly. The National Weather Service will never give you as valid a warning of danger as the Gray Man. If you don't believe it, just ask any of the thousands of people who wouldn't vacation anywhere else.

NORTH ISLAND

The shore at North Island

North Island, South Island, and Cat Island, located at the mouth of Winyah Bay off Georgetown, encompass the twenty thousand acres of marsh, impoundments, ocean beach, pineland, and maritime forest known as the Tom Yawkey Wildlife Center.

North Island consists of 934 acres of upland and 4,449 acres of salt marsh. The northernmost of the three islands, it has hosted many famous visitors, none more noted that the Marquis de Lafayette, who landed here in the fall of 1777, during the Revolutionary War. In fact, it was on North Island that Lafayette first trod American soil. Trying to find a place to dock their boat, he and his party came upon the summer residence of Major Benjamin Huger. The story of Lafayette's unexpected visit was told in May 1779 by Francis Kinloch Huger, Benjamin Huger's son:

> General Lafayette had first landed at my father's home on North Island, in the harbor of Georgetown, in South Carolina. The small vessel in which they had sailed from France made the land off that part of the coast, lying, as they knew, to the north of Charleston, to which port they were bound, but they feared to proceed without information from the city, which might have fallen into the hands of the British during the voyage.
>
> They sent a boat to obtain information, and observing a canoe with Negroes fishing outside the breakers, desired that it might be brought to their vessel. The Negroes in the canoe were people of my father's, who alarmed at observing the boat making for them, endeavored to escape to the shore, but were intercepted and carried on board the vessel; they then piloted the boat with the three gentlemen in it, who were Gen. Lafayette, Baron DeKalb, and (I think) Steuben, to my father's house on the island, which they reached about nightfall.
>
> The first impression of the servants, that it was a privateer's boat, had been communicated to the family, who were soon agreeably relieved from their anxiety. These circumstances were told me by my mother. Their guests remained with them

another day and night, until a carriage and pair of horses could be obtained from the plantation, and my father accompanied them to Charleston.

Lafayette enjoyed his visit with the Hugers. He wrote his wife, back home in France, telling her of the exceptional cordiality with which he and his party were received on North Island and praising the newly proclaimed nation as a whole: "The customs of this world are simple, honest, and altogether worthy of the country where everything reecho[e]s the beautiful name of liberty."

At one time, the Georgetown rice region was almost entirely the domain of the Withers family. James Withers, a Charles Town bricklayer, received a grant of 120 acres near Georgetown in 1736. At his death in 1756, he left four sons: John, Richard, William, and Francis. Between 1764 and 1770, the sons and their mother received grants for about 6,000 acres in the region. Not only did the Witherses own vast plantations, they also had large inventories of madeira wine. They knew how to live well.

The Witherses and their friends summered on North Island. Old letters tell of how Robert Francis Withers, owner of Estherville Plantation on the mainland, sent trusted servants to patrol the beach and guard his family when they were in residence on the island. He stayed with his family on North Island as much as he could, but when it was necessary for him to attend to plantation matters, he was rowed across Winyah Bay by eight slaves.

On September 27 and 28, 1822, a hurricane hit the area. Tides were higher than any in living memory, and Georgetown was seriously damaged. The *Winyaw Intelligencer* estimated that more than

120 blacks and 5 whites were drowned on North Island. Only a small portion of the island remained above water. The storm cost the lives of all the Withers family except Robert Francis Withers.

A remarkable psychic incident preceded the drowning of the family. Years earlier, Sarah Johnston, mother of Mrs. Withers, had dreamed that a storm wiped her family out. After she objected to the family's custom of summering at the beach, the Witherses made arrangements which took them away from the rice fields in the summer, securing residence inland at Stateburg, near Columbia. After Sarah Johnston died in 1817, the family returned to the beach house on North Island each summer until her dream was realized in the storm of 1822.

North Island was so popular as a summer place that some of the planter families rebuilt. A few traces of the aristocracy remain on the island today.

The site of the old Georgetown Light is at the southern end of the island. In 1789, Georgetown planter Paul Trapier made a "gratuitous cession" of land to the federal government for a lighthouse on the bay. Standing eighty-seven feet tall, the light was in operation by 1801. A pair of 1806 hurricanes blew it down, but its replacement continued to guide mariners to the safety of Winyah Bay for years. The North Island Lighthouse is automated today.

Deer abound on the island. After a rain, areas near the sand dunes are covered with tracks. During deer drives around the turn of the century, it was not unusual for thirty deer to be killed in one morning. Ducks were also brought down in large numbers. Everyone desired to be included in a North Island deer drive or duck hunt.

President Grover Cleveland visited the island when it was owned by retired Confederate general Edward Porter Alexander, who entertained in a most lavish manner. A man named Sawney Caines was Cleveland's hunting guide. After the great man had wasted several boxes of shells without doing any harm to the ducks, Caines, not knowing the position Cleveland held, cursed the president as only a Low Country hunting guide could. He took Cleveland's gun and showed him how ducks would fall when properly shot.

The president had a grand time shooting, but he got into trouble when he and his guide were leaving the marsh.

According to Caines, President Cleveland, who weighed at least 250 pounds, was wearing a corduroy suit and hip boots. Caines had acquired the art of walking on marsh mud without sinking, but his guest had no knowledge of the technique. Caines tried to tell the president to put his feet down lightly and walk fast, but Cleveland promptly sank deep in the mud. Caines put his arms under the president's arms and tried to pull him out, but he just sank deeper.

Caines knew he couldn't leave the president stuck in the mud, especially on such a cold day. "It was smack in the middle of a cold spell, in December 1894," he recalled. "I got a good hold and gave a mighty pull. The president's boots stayed in the mud, but I pulled him up on my back and got him back to the boat. That's why that place on North Island is known as the President's Stand."

In 1911, William Yawkey, wealthy industrialist and owner of the Detroit Tigers baseball team, began acquiring property on North, South, and Cat Islands. Among the sportsmen who visited North

Island during his ownership were baseball greats Ty Cobb and Tris Speaker and the governor of South Carolina.

William Yawkey died in 1919 at the age of forty-three. His sole heir was Thomas A. Yawkey, his sixteen-year-old nephew, who thus became the millionaire owner of his uncle's mining, timber, tin, and oil businesses—and the land on South Carolina's sea islands. Like his uncle, Tom Yawkey became a baseball owner. He is fondly remembered today as the longtime patriarch of the Boston Red Sox.

In 1932, Tom Yawkey completed the acquisition of North Island. He valued the property for its "ducking," a term used by Low Country hunters. The island was considered one of the best "ducking" grounds on the Atlantic seaboard, thanks to its preponderance of English and black mallards. On the ocean side of the island, a beach stretched eight miles from North Inlet to the jetty. Turtles laid eggs up and down the beach, and an abundance of sea life—shrimp, crabs, clams, oysters, sheephead, channel bass—was to be gathered from the surrounding waters.

In the late 1930s, Yawkey began developing his island property as a managed waterfowl refuge. The following decade, he created a series of managed marshes by building dikes and trunks. Yawkey was self-taught in matters of wildlife management. From the 1940s to the 1960s, improvements on the islands were largely the result of his trial-and-error experimentation in water levels and salinity. It was in the late 1960s that he began turning the management of his lands over to trained wildlife biologists and their scientific techniques in waterfowl and game management.

Tom Yawkey died in 1976 at the age of seventy-three. In his will, he left North, South, and Cat Islands to the South Carolina

Wildlife Department. He also set up a $10 million trust fund for the perpetual operation of the Tom Yawkey Wildlife Center. Together, the property and the trust fund comprise one of the most outstanding gifts ever given to wildlife conservation in North America.

Today, North Island is a designated wilderness; no activities that would violate its primitive character are permitted. South Island is a waterfowl preserve. The remainder of the property, including Cat Island, is a wildlife management area for migratory birds and native game. Most important, the Tom Yawkey Wildlife Center is, according to its founder's vision, an outdoor laboratory dedicated to new field discoveries and the gradual improvement of wildlife management techniques.

SOUTH ISLAND

South Island is a seven-thousand-acre managed area that was part of the property acquired by Thomas A. Yawkey after his uncle's death. It is bordered by Winyah Bay, the Atlantic Ocean, North Santee Bay, and Mosquito Creek.

The North Santee River bestowed upon the southern side of South Island a natural occurrence important to the production of rice: the twice-daily rise and fall of tidal fresh water. However, the rice produced here was not of the best quality, as salt from ocean water invaded the rice fields. Canals were dug, and rice trunks were installed in the dikes in order to bring water into the fields and allow it to flow away on the outgoing tide.

Although South Island was never as popular a refuge from ma-larial fever as North Island, members of the planter aristocracy did summer here.

South Island played a part in the defense of the mouth of the

North Santee River during the early days of the Civil War. It was important that the planters build defenses along the coast and secure cannons, rifles, shot, powder, and ammunition. There was always danger that the enemy would arrive secretly on the coast. Among those who protected the area were the Georgetown Rifle Guards on redoubts on South and Cat Islands.

After the war, North, South, and Cat Islands became increasingly valuable for their wildlife. In 1936, Rich Knox, the son of slaves, told a story of the most dangerous of South Island's animals:

I was down to the South Island one time and an alligator like to scare me to death. . . .

I was walking across the marsh on South Island, just walking along, not looking down. I saw this big log ahead. Ain't know 'twuz a gator until he raise up. Gator scare me so much that two barrels of gun go off. Shoot all two barrels and have two dead shells in gun. Gator groan at me. Groan at me! Groan like a bull bellow. I look around. See no human. One mind tell me to load up. Shoot him. I take that mind and look at gator. He groan at me. I got him under his shoulder. Groan, bellow, and shake the whole island. Jump up and slap his tail.

I shoot him under the other shoulder. Some say 'sposed to shoot gator on his topknot—bump on the head. He look at 'em and he open his mouth wide. I shoot right down his throat. He not like that. He holler.

I study where I would shoot him again. Shoot him where the tail joins the body. That cut his speed. I study where I can shoot him next. A mind tell me, "Shoot his eye." That weaken him. I shoot seven times. All my shells gone. Gator not dead yet. I lay my gun down. Find an old pole like a cedar pole. I hit that gator a blow. He groan lower. Lower. I left that gator there like a log. Black, ugly, rough, and tough. I still scared most to death of him.

I decide to leave that gator when I thought about the man and his wife coming from church one night. He seen something he thought was a dog. He kicked it. He had kicked a gator. That gator swallow the man's leg right up to his body. Man's foot and shoe down in gator's belly. Wife study. She study what to do. She got down on the gator's back and she took that big old hawk-bill knife outa husband's pocket and rake that knife across gator's throat and pull man outa his stomach. That weaken gator, 'cause under the throat, that is the tenderest place on a gator.

William Yawkey, the uncle of Tom Yawkey, enjoyed fishing and hunting. He constructed a hunting lodge on South Island directly across the bay from the lighthouse on North Island.

Tom Yawkey graduated from Yale in June 1925 and married Elise Starrow, a New York show girl, that same month in a ceremony at the Ritz. A former resident of Birmingham, Alabama, the beautiful Elise had once reigned as Miss Birmingham.

Tom and Elise chose South Island as their winter residence. They built a lovely white Georgian home on a knoll overlooking both water and woods. When construction was completed, however, Tom realized he would never be happy living in such a palatial home. He chose instead the hunting lodge his uncle had constructed on South Island. The Georgian home was turned over to Jim Gibson, the superintendent of South Island Plantation. Elise never spent a night there.

The Yawkeys seemed mismatched. Elise was entertaining, charming, and adept in the social graces. Tom liked to ride and shoot. When word spread that a divorce was imminent, it came as no surprise. Elise filed divorce papers in Reno in November 1944, after a three-year separation. On December 2 of that year, she married businessman Harry Dorsey Watts. On Christmas Eve, Tom married Jean Hollander Hiller in a small wedding at the Georgetown home of Leila and Ralph Ford, Sr. The Fords were dressed to the nines, while the Yawkeys wore hunting clothes purchased at Abercrombie and Fitch in New York. He was forty-one and she was thirty-five.

Tom and Jean arrived on South Island each fall after baseball season ended and remained at the hunting lodge until spring training began in Florida. The lodge burned one summer while the floors were being refinished. The Yawkeys were not in South

Carolina at the time. Informed of the loss, Tom made arrangements for two small mobile homes to be moved to the island. He and Jean lived in the trailers while the superintendent continued to reside in the graceful Georgian home. Tom was noted for his generosity. When asked why he didn't take over the grander home, he replied, "Why, I can't do that! That's the superintendent's house!" The Yawkeys continued to use the trailers as a winter residence until Tom's death. The superintendent resides in the Georgian home to this day.

In the early 1970s, Tom began making frequent trips to the hospital, but the family would not reveal the nature of his illness. At 4:20 P.M. on Friday, July 9, 1976, he died in his sleep at New England Baptist Hospital in Boston, a victim of leukemia. That night, Boston Red Sox players and fans observed a moment of silence as a photo of Yawkey was flashed on the Fenway Park scoreboard. After a private cremation, his ashes were scattered over his beloved islands.

By the end of Yawkey's life, South Island had earned a reputation as one of the most outstanding waterfowl refuges on the Atlantic Flyway. To ensure that his conservation practices would be continued beyond his lifetime, Yawkey bequeathed his islands to the South Carolina Wildlife Department, to be used for wildlife preservation, education, and research. The $10 million trust established by the Yawkey Foundation funds the property's operation. South Island's managed wetlands are maintained for the protection of waterfowl. No duck hunting is permitted.

Following her husband's death, Jean Yawkey became embroiled in a lengthy controversy over control of the Red Sox. A private person, she took up residence at elegant, secluded Mount Pleasant Plantation, located on a high bluff on the Black River within an easy drive of North, South, and Cat Islands. She was still the majority owner of the Red Sox in February 1992, when she died at Massachusetts General Hospital of complications from a stroke. She was eighty-three. Her ashes were also scattered over the sea islands where she and Tom had enjoyed some of their happiest times.

Today's visitors to South Island might enjoy the 1996 movie *Fly Away Home*. Starring Anna Paquin and Jeff Daniels, it concerns a young girl who becomes a mother to newly hatched goslings and uses an ultralight airplane to teach them how to migrate.

The movie was based on the adventures of Bill Lishman, a Canadian metal sculptor who made ornithological and aviation history when he raised a flock of young geese to "imprint" on him and his ultralight—meaning that the geese considered him their mother and would follow him anywhere. To test the premise that he could use an ultralight to teach imprinted geese a safe migration route, Lishman, working with scientist William Sladen of Virginia, led flocks of geese from his home in Ontario to the Tom Yawkey Wildlife Center in 1994 and 1995. Some of the spectators who witnessed the landings at the center were rendered speechless by the sight of a flock of geese in perfect **V** formation following an ultralight.

CAT ISLAND

Cat Island

The Santees, the Waccamaws, and other Native Americans of the Sioux nation once populated North, South, and Cat Islands, but they didn't survive the European onslaught.

By 1721, Georgetown was a permanent settlement. It became a port of entry a few years later. The planters created an agrarian district which extended along the four great rivers—the

Waccamaw, the Pee Dee, the Black, and the Sampit—that empty into the Atlantic Ocean between the barrier islands.

Alexander Hume established a plantation on the western side of Cat Island during the 1700s. Hume Plantation contained a thousand acres, four hundred of which were prime tidal swamp and a hundred of which were used for growing food. The property included a twelve-room residence, an extensive kitchen, a carriage house, an overseer's house, stables, and accommodations for 150 slaves. The manor house was surrounded by live oaks. Today, an old grave site can be seen on the former Hume Plantation. The last person buried there was laid to rest in 1852.

Another plantation on Cat Island was White Marsh, owned by William Rivers Maxwell (1794–1873). In 1850, Maxwell's acreage produced six hundred thousand pounds of rice.

Traces of plantation life remain on Cat Island, including an avenue of live oaks and a bamboo stand. The plantations all seemed to have a stand of bamboo—perhaps because everyone in residence needed a fishing pole.

When Thomas A. Yawkey acquired his Cat Island holdings, a settlement of slave descendants was living on the property. Those residents wanted a place of worship, so Yawkey built St. James A.M.E. Church.

St. James holds the distinction of being one of the few small churches in the world that has hosted a visit by the archbishop of Canterbury. He and his wife visited the island years ago and asked to go inside the church. Their eyes took in the handmade wooden furnishings and pasteboard fans. They marveled at the small, isolated place of worship so unlike Canterbury Cathedral.

Regular services were held at St. James until a modern ferry replaced the old cable ferry. After frequent breakdowns of the new ferry stranded some members, attendance declined. Eventually, church services were discontinued. Today, a cornerstone recognizes the generosity of the Yawkeys in their gift of St. James A.M.E. Church.

According to a story told by a reporter with the *Charleston News and Courier*, Yawkey's islands were so frequently without electricity that he decided to have a diesel generator constructed for South Island. He contacted a Westinghouse engineer, who came to the island and looked over the situation. Yawkey explained that the generator would have to be transported to the island by barge, as the ferry could not support it. The engineer disputed Yawkey. He said he knew exactly what he was going to build, and that it could go across on the ferry to Cat Island, then on to South Island by road.

Unable to talk the engineer out of his plan, Yawkey invited friends, newspaper reporters, and others to a party on the day of the generator's arrival. He explained to them that they would witness the ferry and generator sink on their way to Cat Island. The party gathered by the Intracoastal Waterway, dining on steak, oysters, and champagne. When the flatbed truck arrived with the generator, Yawkey gave the engineer one last chance to deliver it to the island by barge, but the man refused and climbed aboard the ferry. Sure enough, the ferry began to sink in midstream. Yawkey called out, "Go down with the boat. Every good captain goes down with his boat!"

After Yawkey's death, his widow, Jean, realized there were two things her husband had most desired: he wanted the Boston Red Sox to win the World Series, and he wanted to acquire the rest of Cat Island to assure the future integrity of the area. In conjunction with the South Carolina Nature Conservatory, Jean Yawkey was able to acquire additional lands. Today, North, South, and Cat Islands all bear the protection of the Tom Yawkey Wildlife Center. Unfortunately, Red Sox fans are still waiting for that World Series title.

Cat Island remains a haven for wildlife. Guests are amazed by the black fox squirrels, which are twice as large as more common gray squirrels. Ospreys arrive near Valentine's Day and use the same nests year after year, always on an open perch. As for the duck population, an estimated five thousand pintails, three thousand widgeons, and fifteen hundred teals utilized Cat Island's ponds in 1995–96. They were just part of the Tom Yawkey Wildlife Center's total population of thirty-five thousand ducks, which winter primarily on South Island. Bald eagles reside on Cat Island's four active nest sites each winter; an additional fifteen juvenile birds utilize the wildlife center during the cold months. It is said that rattlesnakes on Cat Island come in two sizes: as big around as your arm and as big around as your leg.

The sixty-five miles of dirt roadways at the center meander under oaks, through expansive longleaf-pine forests, and in sight of miles and miles of abandoned rice fields now reverted to marsh. Educational field trips are conducted weekly by the resident biologist, Bob Joyner, who also tells colorful tales of the islands. The center is operated in a manner in keeping with Tom Yawkey's wish for the islands. Attention is given to historic sites and the ecology of the various habitats.

Bulls Island entered recorded history on St. Patrick's Day 1670, when two English ships loaded with settlers dropped anchor in Bulls Harbor, a wide inlet that afforded safe anchorage and access to fresh water. They were greeted by canoes full of Seewee Indians. The Indians had four or five small villages on the mainland, located across the wide marsh. The Indians called the island Hunting Island.

The first English owner of the island was John Collins, a member of a family that migrated to South Carolina from Barbados. The island was granted to Collins by the Lords Proprietors. In his will of 1707, John Collins left his mainland plantation, Tibwin, and the island to his son Alexander. At Alexander's death, his brother Jonah came into possession of both tracts. The island even-

The shore at Bulls Island

tually passed from the Collins family to the Bull family, another prominent colonial line. Bulls Island took its new name from that family.

In reaction to continuing harassment by pirates, the colonial House of Commons authorized the construction of several forts along the coast. One—a wooden upper structure resting on a tabby foundation—was built on Bulls Island.

During the Revolutionary War, British marauders landed on the island and torched all its buildings. Other unfriendly visits came during the War of 1812 and the Civil War. On one occasion during the Civil War, a Union gunboat ran the shallow channel at the eastern end of Bulls Bay and then steamed up Five Fathom Creek.

At the end of the war, the Reconstruction government tried to persuade freed slaves to settle here, but they rejected the offer.

The Magwood family held the island until 1921, when it was bought by wealthy sportsman Gayer B. Dominick of New York City. Dominick built a large plantation-style lodge on the island and used it for winter hunting. After he conveyed the island to the United States Fish and Wildlife Service in 1936, the lodge was used by visitors, especially ornithologists and amateur bird watchers.

During World War II, Bulls Island became—for a few hours, at least—a center of concern for the Department of Defense. A unit of the Coast Guard's shore patrol was stationed on the island. Its men had a telephone line along the beach and patrolled on horseback. They had been briefed about the two-man submarines the Germans had developed for penetrating harbor defenses.

At about one o'clock one morning, a young Coast Guardsman was riding his horse on the island when he heard what he took to be a steam valve releasing pressure. He was able to make out long, low shapes on the reef. Spurring his mount to the first field telephone, he told the command at Dominick House what he had seen and heard. The message was relayed by radio to the Charleston Naval Base and then transmitted to Department of Defense headquarters in Washington, D.C.

Just before the president was notified, the first light of dawn revealed the source of the emergency to be sixty-five pilot whales that had come ashore in one of their mysterious beachings. So ended the military emergency.

"Of these [South Carolina] islands, I know Bulls Island best," said the late Dr. Archibald Rutledge, former owner of Hampton

Plantation and beloved poet laureate of South Carolina. From the beach at Bulls Island, Rutledge once witnessed an escape he found both dramatic and poetic.

It was sunrise on a January morning. Some deer poachers had been on the island the week before and in their hasty departure had left behind a great black hound. Suddenly, Rutledge heard the deep tones of the hound mingling with the pounding surf. Out of the thickets, a great stag with a heavy crown of antlers burst upon the beach. Behind him was the black hound. Rutledge stood wondering if the stag could be pulled down by a strong dog. If the stag stayed on the beach, he would surely be caught, Rutledge believed. But the stag turned toward the surf just as the sun appeared over the ocean. Dashing through the sparkling shallows, he plunged into deeper water. A huge wave broke over him, momentarily hiding him from view.

And what of the hound? It tried to pursue the stag but discovered it had no relish for the sea. Crestfallen, it retreated to the beach and sat facing the ocean. It had not only lost its prey but had been outwitted as well. It was a scene Rutledge never forgot.

Such wild scenes are far from uncommon on the island. At 5,018 acres, Bulls Island is the largest island in Cape Romain National Wildlife Refuge, its closest competitors being Cape Island and Raccoon Key. The only wooded island in the refuge, Bulls provides the most diversified habitat for mammals. Eight impoundments on the island create freshwater marshes covering about 990 acres. The extensive salt marshes on the western side of the island are protected from the pounding waves of the ocean. A maritime forest consisting primarily of live oaks, loblolly pines, and cabbage palmettos occupies about 1,500 acres of the island's interior. Sand dunes also provide habitat for mammals, as does the salt-spray forest community. Wildlife clearings and firebreaks provide about 40 acres of old-field habitat.

Bulls Island is probably best known for its red wolf breeding program. Red wolves were reintroduced to the island under the Endangered Species Act in 1973. These animals are mostly brown- and buff-colored, with some black along their backs; there is sometimes a reddish color behind their ears and toward the back of their legs. They are intermediate in size between gray wolves and coyotes. The average adult male weighs sixty-one pounds. Adult red wolves are about twenty-six inches long from nose to tail.

The Bulls Island program began in November 1987, when a male and a female red wolf arrived from Point Defiance Zoo in Tacoma, Washington, and were placed in a pen for breeding. Three pups were born in the spring of 1988. In July of that year, the adult male and female and two male pups were released on the island. The next month, the female was found dead, apparently killed by an alligator. The adult male assumed total responsibility for rearing the pups.

A new female arrived from Tacoma in the fall. In the spring of 1989, five female pups were born. Again, the adult female was killed by an alligator; one of her pups was also killed. After Hurricane Hugo that fall, the adult male was found dead, apparently from injuries sustained during the hurricane. A new adult male arrived from Gulf Island National Seashore in January.

And so the program continued, a mix of successes and failures. In June 1993, the wolves were fitted with transmitters for tracking. Today, a pair of red wolves and its pups live in the wild on the island. They are no threat to visitors. The animals are shy and secretive. Even experts rarely catch a glimpse of them.

There are times when Bulls Island is open for archery hunting. George E. Campsen, Jr., recorded the first kill of the modern Bulls Island archery hunts in 1956.

Cape Romain National Wildlife Refuge maintains headquarters at Moore's Landing on Seewee Bay. Established in 1932, the refuge encompasses 34,229 acres of land and 30,000 acres of water, all of it closed to migratory waterfowl hunting. It is one of only two federal reserves with a Class One wilderness rating, the highest possible classification. Though the rating is indicative of the pristine air and water in the refuge, it does not apply to Bulls Island because of its hiking trails and vehicle access.

The refuge is home to 277 species of birds, 12 species of amphibians, 24 species of reptiles, and 36 species of mammals. It is a popular spot among bird watchers and shell collectors. Visitors depart from Moore's Landing, located off U.S. 17 seventy-five miles south of Myrtle Beach. The *Island Cat*, a thirty-eight-passenger pontoon ferry, makes the trip to Bulls Island several days each week. Call 803-881-4582 for more information.

ISLE OF PALMS

Oceanfront residences on the Isle of Palms

The Isle of Palms, formerly known as Long Island, was once owned by two brothers named Swinton. One brother planted and cultivated oysters and the other raised cattle. The Swintons also owned neighboring Little Goat Island, Big Goat Island, Pine Island, and Club House Island, which they obtained in 1732 in a grant from King George II.

A resolution was passed in 1791 allowing citizens to build houses on the Isle of Palms. In 1796, property was assessed, commissioners appointed, streets laid out, and Sunday gambling prohibited. Between 1798 and 1821, Hibben's Ferry gave Charlestonians access to the island.

Two violent hurricanes crashed on the South Carolina coast during 1893, one on August 27 and the other on Friday, October 13. The Isle of Palms suffered along with the rest of the coastal area. Hundreds of people lost their lives. Houses washed to sea while their inhabitants sat inside. A headline in the Atlanta paper read, "THE WHOLE ATLANTIC WAS SCARED."

Near the end of the century, the Isle of Palms was sold to Dr. Joseph H. Lawrence, who saw its possibilities as a resort and organized the Charleston Seashore and Railroad Company. The first passengers were taken over the eight miles of railroad on July 28, 1898. The train crossed Cove Inlet on a long trestle with a swing bridge. By the summer of 1899, thousands of people were pouring onto the island for vacations and holidays. An all-you-can-eat dinner was served at a local restaurant for fifty cents.

One of the attractions was an amusement park with a ferris wheel, a carousel complete with brass ring, and other entertainments. A favorite ride was the "Steeple Chase," imported from Coney Island. Its five mechanical horses raced around a U-shaped course, the winner receiving a free ride. From a distance, the ride looked like a roller coaster.

Railroad excursions brought tourists from Columbia and Augusta. They had to get up long before day in order to catch a morning train to Charleston, ride a trolley to the ferry, then ride another trolley on the Isle of Palms for a dip in the ocean before lunch. Charleston County took over the ferry operation before service finally ended in 1919.

An upturn in tourism came in 1936, when retail merchants on the island estimated a 20 percent increase in business over the previous year. During the next year, hotels, always a barometer of good times, showed an increase in business of about 37 percent.

Not least among the attractions offered at the Isle of Palms that year was the Big Apple, the newest dance craze. The dance—created in Columbia at the Big Apple Club by Elliott Wright, the club's 350-pound manager—was done by from five to twenty couples arranged in a circle. Some tourists had so much fun that they began to look at the Isle of Palms as a place to live year-round. By 1938, oceanfront lots were advertised for sale for two thousand dollars.

When J. C. Long bought the island in 1944, only about a dozen houses were there. As development progressed, well-to-do white people began to move to the island. Today, only a few black families own property on the Isle of Palms, where high property taxes and real-estate prices and an expensive lifestyle are the order of the day.

In September 1989, Hurricane Hugo took a heavy toll on local property. Homes were damaged, trees were downed, and severe erosion plagued the strand. The Isle of Palms had a hard time living up to its name after so much greenery was blown away. But a local volunteer group changed that with a $200,000 landscaping project aimed at planting palm trees up and down Palm Boulevard, the island's main thoroughfare. The "Plant a Palm on Palm Committee"—whose membership included Peatsy Hollings, the wife of United States senator Ernest F. Hollings of South Carolina—inspired residents to contribute money to help with the landscaping.

Today, the Isle of Palms remains a popular resort. It is the site of many outstanding oceanfront residences and is the home of the Wild Dunes Resort, famous for its golfing and boating facilities.

SULLIVAN'S ISLAND

Sullivan's Island lighthouse

When a popular author left her country-club lifestyle and moved to Sullivan's Island several years ago to "live off the sea," some people asked how she could do such a thing. But with gridlock on the highways and long lines in the cities, it isn't difficult to see why she chose a simpler life on an island across the harbor from Charleston.

One look at Sullivan's Island and it's clear that even the old houses were built with sea breezes in mind, so as to catch a wind blowing from any direction. The bedrooms are situated at the corners of the house, each one built almost as a separate entity, with windows on all four sides. Picture a rectangular house with a tiny, square house attached at each corner.

Sullivan's Island, which spans an area approximately three miles long and one mile wide and is represented on most maps as an inconspicuous dot off Charleston, may be the state's original seaside resort.

The island was discovered in July 1666 by Captain Robert Sandford. Eight years later, Captain Florentia O'Sullivan, a deputy to one of the Lords Proprietors, was placed in command of the island. O'Sullivan's duties consisted of manning a "great gun," which was "to be fired upon the approach of any ship or ships." The point at the harbor's eastern entrance was selected as the gun's position. The property became known as O'Sullivan's Island, later corrupted to Sullivan's Island.

In O'Sullivan's day, it was not unusual for settlers to find themselves short of rations. Island residents in the area around Charles Town came to be known as "Sand Crabs," while mainlanders were called "Hungry Necks." The two groups competed spiritedly over foodstuffs brought in from England.

In 1718, the island's guns defended Charles Town when pirates were harassing the coast. On December 10 of that year, the notorious pirate Stede Bonnet attempted to take refuge from Colonel William Rhett but was captured after a bloody fight on the upper end of the island during which one pirate was killed. Tried in Charles Town, twenty-nine of Bonnet's crewmen were hanged there. Their bodies were left dancing for several days as an example to those sympathetic to piracy. Stede Bonnet was tried two days later. Found guilty, he was dragged in a hurdle to the place of execution. A noose was dropped around Bonnet's neck, and he was swung off the cart.

The history of South Carolina's state flag is intertwined with that of Sullivan's Island. In 1775, Colonel William Moultrie was directed by the Council of Safety to provide a state flag. He chose the color of the uniforms of the First and Second Regiments for the field of blue. On this, he arranged the silver crescent which adorned the soldiers' hats. But the palmetto tree was not added until after Moultrie's successful defense of a little, unfinished, crudely made fort on Sullivan's Island during the Revolutionary War.

In June 1776, word reached South Carolina that Sir Peter Parker and his massive fleet were heading south from New York for the purpose of making Charles Town a base for British operations. While Charles Town patriots tore down waterfront warehouses to clear a path for cannon fire, Moultrie was given the task of constructing a fort on the southern tip of Sullivan's Island. His men built double walls of thick palmetto planks with a layer of sand between them. Three walls were raised by the time the British arrived. Moultrie's efforts notwithstanding, most observers considered the harbor defense futile in the face of the great invading fleet.

On the morning of June 16, over three hundred British cannons were fired simultaneously at the fort. The officers of the fleet waited for the smoke to clear, confident that the fort had been shattered. To their astonishment, they saw that the spongy palmetto logs had simply soaked up their cannonballs without apparent damage. When Moultrie's turn came, he began the counterattack that left the British fleet in tatters by the end of the day. Sir Peter Parker was even wounded in the buttocks by flying splinters.

It was during this engagement that Sir William Jasper performed his famed deed of jumping over the palmetto walls and setting aright the flag, which had been shot down.

In the wake of the battle, it seemed only fitting that the palmetto tree should be added to the state flag and that the fort should bear the name of Colonel Moultrie, its gallant defender. The palmetto tree has since become symbolic of the British defeat at Sullivan's Island.

By the time President George Washington made his Southern tour in 1791, the fort was in ruins. It was rebuilt before being destroyed by a hurricane in 1804.

By 1809, a brick Fort Moultrie was constructed. It still stands today. Sergeant Edgar Allen Poe was once stationed here. His story

Fort Moultrie

"The Gold Bug" reveals his impressions of the island. Poe arrived as a private in November 1827. His stay at Fort Moultrie lasted a year. During that time, he established a reputation as an intense young man who was fond of walking the beach during storms.

Another famous visitor to Sullivan's Island was Osceola, the chief of the Seminoles, who arrived with a party of a hundred warriors, women, and children. They were taken to Fort Moultrie, where Osceola became ill and died in January 1838. His grave lies at the foot of the northern wall of the fort.

When the North and South became openly hostile in December 1860, Major Robert Anderson ordered Fort Moultrie evacuated and moved his troops to nearby Fort Sumter, an action that helped bring on the Civil War. Although Anderson's men attempted to disable Fort Moultrie, the Confederates used it to help make Fort Sumter an unhappy place for Union troops. The men at Moultrie fought a Federal ironclad and other battles before the fort was deserted in February 1865. Visitors to Fort Moultrie can still see traces of that earlier era.

Across the street from the fort is a United States Coast Guard station and its lighthouse. If you look closely, you will notice a bunker next to the lighthouse. During World War II, many such bunkers were constructed around the island to protect a receiving station commanded by the late George Marshall, then a colonel. After the war, some enterprising souls bought the bunkers and turned them into underground homes. The homes have been featured in various newspapers and magazines and are an interesting feature of Sullivan's Island. The northeastern portion of the island is still known as "the Marshall Reservation."

Sullivan's Island was considered a desirable place to live even before World War II. Second-row lots were priced at nine hundred dollars in 1937. In those days, Charleston folk who summered at Sullivan's saw about as many horses riding the breakers as people. Taking horses to the beach was the rage; when people went swimming, their horses went, too.

The island saw a burst of popularity in the 1970s that hasn't slowed since. Today, it remains a hit both as a summer resort—refreshingly, one with no high-rise hotels—and a place of year-round residence.

FORT SUMTER

Fort Sumter

Fort Sumter is on a small island in Charleston Harbor. Named for General Thomas Sumter, the "Gamecock of the Revolution," the fort was begun in 1829 but was still unfinished in 1860 when South Carolina seceded from the United States.

At that time, there were four Federal installations around Charleston Harbor: Fort Moultrie on Sullivan's Island; Castle

Pinckney on Shutes Folly Island; Fort Johnson on James Island, across from Moultrie; and Fort Sumter at the harbor entrance. The only post garrisoned by more than a trifling number of soldiers was Fort Moultrie, where Major Robert Anderson commanded two companies of the First United States Artillery.

Six days after the secession ordinance, Anderson concluded that Moultrie was indefensible and transferred the Federal troops to Fort Sumter, a mile away. Confederate forces soon manned the other installations. Thus, South Carolina had seceded from the Union, but Federals occupied a strategic fort at the entrance of Charleston Harbor. The South demanded that Fort Sumter be vacated. The North refused.

As the weeks passed, Fort Sumter became the focal point of tensions between North and South. When Abraham Lincoln assumed office as president of the United States in early 1861, he made it clear that he would uphold national authority. On April 4, Lincoln ordered that merchant steamers protected by ships of war carry supplies to Major Anderson. On April 11, Confederate general P. G. T. Beauregard demanded that Anderson surrender Fort Sumter. Anderson refused.

For days, Charleston sat in wait for the commencement of hostilities. Public suspense was at its height. Troops, munitions, and stores were being carried to the fortifications in the harbor.

At 2:00 P.M. on April 11, General Beauregard again demanded the surrender of Fort Sumter. Dispatches between Anderson and Beauregard continued during the afternoon and night.

Finally, at 3:20 A.M. on April 12, Confederate forces informed Anderson that their batteries would open fire in one hour. Captain George S. James, commanding Fort Johnson's eastern mortar battery, ordered the firing of a signal shell. The sound woke all camps.

Major Anderson found himself facing 6,000 Confederates. His garrison at Fort Sumter numbered only 90 soldiers, though the fort was designed for 650 men. He simply didn't have the manpower to crew his five dozen guns, most of which remained unfired throughout the historic battle.

Not so the Confederate cannons, which sent more than three thousand shells—some of them weighing forty-two pounds—toward Fort Sumter over the next thirty-four hours. The one-sided battle finally ended around 1:30 P.M. on April 13. Anderson surrendered that evening. Miraculously, no one on either side was killed during the engagement.

According to the generous surrender terms, Anderson and his men were allowed to leave Fort Sumter with all their personal possessions—including small arms—and sail for New York City. They were even allowed to fire a salute to the United States flag as it was lowered from its staff. Unfortunately, the guns ignited a piece of cloth, which landed in a pile of unfired cartridges, setting off an explosion that sent masonry and pieces of cannon flying. One Union soldier died on the scene and another after being taken to a Charleston hospital. The only fatalities at Fort Sumter were thus the victims of military ritual, not battle.

Since Charleston was an important port for Confederate blockade runners as the war progressed, it remained a prominent Union target. The Union army tried to take Charleston in June 1862 but failed and withdrew. On April 7, 1863, the Federal navy attacked Fort Sumter and Charleston with a large force of ironclads, only to be defeated. That summer, the Union took control of

Folly Island, beginning the long siege of Charleston. Fort Sumter was finally abandoned in 1865, when Federal troops occupied the area from the rear.

Today, the little island facing the open sea is clearly visible from the Charleston Battery. Boats take visitors to the island from locations in Charleston Harbor. Government caretakers show visitors battle-scarred walls where guns were mounted. The inner fortifications have been carefully restored, but the outer walls are mostly original.

Field hands who worked the cotton on James Island, across the harbor from Charleston, firmly believed in ghosts, "hants," and "hags." A James Island preacher once told his congregation that he took "no stock in conjure and such like," then went on to assert his beliefs in hants and hags. He had seen plenty of them, he said, "'specially on the new moon." According to the preacher, hants looked like the shadow of a person at night. Hags, on the other hand, were real humans who slipped out of their skin at midnight to vex people, then had to be back in their skin at first crow.

There were residents who even believed there was a ghost town on the island. Sometimes, when the mist rolled in from the sea, they claimed to be able to view the profile of New Towne in the vicinity of Stono Creek. New Towne was one of the earliest settlements on James Island.

One supernatural happening took place during slave days on the small bit of land known as Solomon Legare Island, now part of James Island. Phyllis Green, a slave, was asked by her mistress whether she thought the slaves were better off in the United States than in Africa, since they were taught religion and improved ways of living in their new home. Green replied, "I ain't know, cause them as could fly flew home."

As Green told the story, a slave owner had brought over a new batch of slaves from Africa. According to the custom of the time, the group was given two weeks in which to adjust to the new surroundings before being set to work. But these were not ordinary beings. "When they [were] left by theyself you could hear a tapping, tapping, tapping, all day and all night," Green said. "And they wouldn't crack their teeth to them [would not speak to anyone]."

Finally, the time came for the slave driver to call them to work with the crack of his whip. "They come out and they stretch out their hands just like they going to take the tools to work like the rest," Green said. "But when they stretch their hands they rise. At middle day, you could see them far out over the ocean. At sundown, you could hear voices, but they couldn't see them no more. They gone home."

It was in December 1671 that the ships *Blessing* and *Phoenix* arrived at Charles Town with a group of settlers from the recently conquered Dutch province of Nova Belgia, henceforth to be called New York. The names of some of the settlers—Smith, Miller—suggest they were not Dutchmen but Englishmen who had settled temporarily in the Dutch colony.

As recorded in the *Journals of the Grand Council* on December 20, a settlement was established as follows: "It is advised and resolved that thirty acres of land be laid out most convenient to the water for landing in a place on a Creeke Southward from Stono Creeke for a Towne for the settlement of those persons who lately arrived from New Yorke which said Town shall be called and known by the name of James Towne."

Alternately known as New Towne, James Towne—named for King James II—was located on high land on the island.

The opening shots of the Civil War were fired from Fort Johnson, built on James Island in 1708 and expanded in 1737. More than three thousand shells were thrown at Fort Sumter over the course of a thirty-four-hour bombardment before Union major Robert Anderson agreed to the terms stipulated by Confederate general P. G. T. Beauregard and surrendered under honorable conditions.

There is little left of Fort Johnson today. Its ninety-acre tract was turned over to the College of Charleston and the Medical College of South Carolina for research use in 1952. The property is now jointly owned. The College of Charleston maintains its Marine Biological Laboratory on the site, while the South Carolina Wildlife Commission operates the Marine Research Laboratory.

One thing visitors can see on the site is Marshlands Plantation House, built by John Ball on the Cooper River around 1810. Marshlands served as officers' quarters at the Charleston Naval

Base until 1961, when the United States Navy decided that the site it occupied was needed for other purposes. It was then acquired by the College of Charleston and moved by water to its present location. Many people came to watch the manor house making its way across the Cooper and Ashley Rivers.

After the Civil War, the James Island planters realized the need for unity of action if they were to survive. A large assembly met at the residence of William G. Hinson on July 4, 1872, and appointed a committee to draw up a constitution. Less than a year later, the James Island Agricultural Society was born.

The object of the society, as set forth in its constitution, was "the development of agriculture upon the seaboard of our state." Applicants for membership had to either live on or own property on James Island. The society later became so influential along the coast that people from other sections wanted to become members. The James Islanders then amended the constitution to

Marshlands Plantation House

allow outsiders to become members if they proved their sincere interest in agriculture.

The first official act of the president was to appoint three members to the Agricultural Committee, later known as the Riding Committee. It was the committeemen's duty to ride the land of all members during the last week in June to find out the number of acres that each had planted, the kind of fertilizer used, the method of cultivation, and the date of planting. In October, the committeemen rode again. After the harvest, they got from each member a written statement of the yield per acre. Members attended meetings of agricultural societies in neighboring communities. They even started a library with the purchase of a number of books on agriculture and stock.

Cotton was the principal crop on James Island, though acreage was also devoted to corn, sweet potatoes, and forage crops. The average cotton crop was about fifty acres. Sea-island cotton required much more time, attention, and labor than the short cotton in cultivation in the inland portion of the state, and the acreage was necessarily smaller. When the James Islanders discovered that planting cotton on land that had previously been pasture gave a better product, they purchased stock, pastured half the land, and planted the other half.

In 1882 began a series of bad years. First appeared a cotton disease called "black arm" or "rust," which made the cotton die early. The next year, the farmers cut down on their cotton acreage and began planting larger truck crops and using commercial fertilizers. Then, almost overnight, hordes of caterpillars destroyed all the crops on the island. In 1885, a hurricane visited James Island, and acres of cotton were swept away. In 1893 came another hurricane as well as blight, which threatened to put an end to the cotton industry.

Just when agricultural pursuits on James Island seemed doomed, something good happened. On July 4, 1900, E. L. Rivers, one of the island's most outstanding planters, reported that he had finally succeeded in developing a cotton seed that was blight-proof. His achievement was recognized by the United States Department of Agriculture and *Encyclopedia Britannica*. The old days of sea-island cotton production were resurrected. Prices were high. Cotton sold for between $.75 and $1.50 a pound, and potatoes brought the unheard-of price of $14.00 per barrel.

In 1919, disaster struck harder than ever, as the boll weevil brought down the final curtain on sea-island cotton. The boll weevil is said to have been as destructive to the South as the Civil War. Things were so bad on James Island that a story was told of a man who was riding beside a cotton field one day when he heard a noise he didn't understand. He stopped and walked into the field to investigate, only to find an old boll weevil whipping a young one because it wasn't carrying two rows at a time.

The boll weevil ended sea-island cotton culture on the island, but it didn't kill the famous James Island Agricultural Society. Each year on the Fourth of July, residents gather for an anniversary meeting. Thankfully for the local ladies, the men-only rule has been relaxed.

Recent years have brought many changes in the agricultural life of James Island. Some of the old cotton plantations have been turned into dairy and truck farms. Farmers raise vegetables for the Northern market and sell milk in Charleston. Suburban development has spread over other plantations, but some of the old churches have endured, such as James Island Presbyterian Church.

A not-to-be-missed attraction on James Island is the tombstone of Sammy Smalls, located near James Island Presbyterian Church. Before the Civil War, the church had two cemeteries, one for whites and the other for blacks. But "Goat Cart Sammy" Smalls, the crippled beggar who was DuBose Heyward's inspiration for the character Porgy in his novel of the same name, was buried in neither.

Porgy achieved immortality, but the real Sammy Smalls accumulated a stack of police citations. Records show that he shot at least two women, neither of them Normie, the basis for the character Bess. When Smalls died, it was deemed appropriate to lay him to rest on James Island, which he called Jim Island. But as an unrepentant sinner, he was not privileged to inhabit a grave in sanctified ground. It was Normie who laid him to rest outside the small graveyard. Because of his unrepentant status, Smalls was buried "crossways of the world"—that is, north-south rather than east-west. His goat died shortly after Sammy's burial. The goat "didn't eat nothin' after Sammy gone," Normie told Major Henry F. Church, who sketched Sammy. "He just grieve and die. He want to be wid Sammy." Church's work hung in the venerated halls of Milan's La Scala opera house when *Porgy and Bess* was presented there.

Visitors can reach the community of Folly Beach by traveling across James Island, going over the bridge to Folly Island, and continuing to the ocean. George Gershwin lived in an oceanfront cottage at 708 West Arctic Avenue on this beach during part of

The tombstone of Sammy Smalls

the time he was writing his great folk opera *Porgy and Bess*, based on DuBose Heyward's *Porgy*. Initially, Gershwin didn't want to leave New York and his work at Radio City Music Hall to come to South Carolina, and Heyward didn't want to leave Charleston. They corresponded for a time before Gershwin finally decided the trip south would be worth it. In December 1933, he came to Charleston. Then, in the summer of 1934, he and his cousin Henry Botkin moved to Folly Beach.

Heyward remembered the impact that the area had on Gershwin. "James Island, with its large population of Gullah

Negroes, furnished us with a laboratory in which to test our theories, as well as an inexhaustible source of folk material," he noted. "But the interesting discovery to me, as we sat listening to their moving spirituals, or watched a group shuffling before a country store or cabin, was that it was more like a homecoming to George than an exploration."

As he listened to the strains of the island music, Gershwin received the inspiration for the stirring, haunting "Summertime," "Bess, You Is My Woman Now," and other classics.

By 1937, Folly Beach was a lively place. Ads for galas ran regularly in the *Charleston News and Courier*. For an admission charge of twenty cents, people could attend an afternoon concert and evening amateur contests. The Original Dixieland Swing Band played, and tap-dancers and song-and-dance teams were additional attractions.

In June 1943, the collection of tolls on Folly Beach Road ceased, ending a practice of twenty years' standing. On the day of the "Freedom Party" celebration, a motorcade left Charleston's Marion Square and arrived at the toll gate about four o'clock in the afternoon. State Senator Oliver T. Wallace purchased the last ticket on Folly Beach Road as taps was sounded. A parade of cars proceeded to Folly Beach to enjoy a variety of entertainment.

Plans to burn the tollhouse were abandoned when a Folly Beach resident offered to buy the structure for fifty dollars for use as a bathhouse.

Morris Island, a small island off James Island, is the site from which a group of Citadel cadets shelled a ship bearing supplies for Union forces at Fort Sumter more than three months before the Civil War began. Union troops laid siege to Morris Island in 1863.

Morris Island was also the place where the remains of the *Ruby* came to rest after her encounter with the USS *Proteus*. The *Ruby* was one of the most successful blockade runners based in the area. Beginning in early 1862, she plied the waters between Charleston and Nassau. It was not until February 27, 1865, that she ran afoul of Commander R. W. Shuffeldt and the *Proteus*, whose bombardment shattered the *Ruby*'s hull and left it to wash ashore on Morris Island. It was for taking such risks that blockade runners received $5,000 a month, instead of the $150 that had been the prevailing rate in the merchant service before the war. "Charlestonians never looked down on blockade-runners," said Jack Leland, former managing editor of the *Charleston News and Courier*. "They wouldn't have had anything during that war had it not been for the blockade-runners."

Morris Island's 150-foot lighthouse, listed on the National Register of Historic Places, was built in 1876. It was the third lighthouse on the site. The first was erected in 1767.

The island has eroded by more than thirty-five hundred feet since the beginning of the twentieth century, and the lighthouse now stands a thousand feet out in the sea.

The Coast Guard abandoned the structure as surplus government property in the 1960s. It passed through a series of private owners before Robert New, a resident of Folly Beach, proposed that a commission buy the lighthouse to keep it in public hands. An engineering firm then suggested that a watertight structure be built below the lighthouse to protect it.

The future of the structure remains uncertain. The lighthouse has a four-foot-thick brick base. The water is about ten feet deep at the base at low tide.

Unfortunately, Morris Island is but one example of the widespread erosion affecting the beaches of Charleston County today. The barrier islands from the Isle of Palms to Seabrook Island are losing sand. Some blame the jetties built in Charleston Harbor in the late nineteenth century for the loss of sand on Morris Island and the erosion problems at Folly Beach, claiming that the jetties and the dredging of the channel have kept sand from reaching the islands to the south. Only time will tell the future of the area's beaches.

JOHNS ISLAND

When the Reverend Stono, a Presbyterian minister, headed toward Charles Town Harbor aboard the *Rising Sun*, he believed he would be in the city only long enough to bring supplies aboard. He didn't know that a hurricane was about to overtake him and founder his ship off the Charles Town bar. While stranded in Charles Town, he was offered a pastorate there. He accepted the call.

After becoming established in the area, Stono began organizing churches on the barrier islands. Johns Island Presbyterian Church was founded around 1710 under his leadership. Many parishioners were wealthy, having large plantations on the island and elegant townhouses in Charles Town. They not only contributed funds to build a fine church but remembered the minister in their wills, calling for the interest from their investments to be used for his maintenance.

The sanctuary of Johns Island Presbyterian Church was framed of hand-sawed heart pine, held together by wooden pegs. The roof was made of hand-split black-cypress shingles. Bricks for the foundation were brought from England.

The sanctuary, believed to have been built in 1719, was enlarged in 1823. After the Civil War, the members offered the use of their church to local Episcopalians as long as they needed it. For a time, the Episcopalians held services on the first and third Sundays of the month and the Presbyterians on the second and fourth Sundays.

Members took a great deal of pride in their church. The Ladies Working Society raised money for the splendid iron fence around the grounds. Before it was installed, Mrs. Francis Y. Legare, Sr., was asked if bids would be solicited for the work. "Bids!" she replied. "The women have been working for this fence for over two years, and I don't expect to pay one cent to put it up. I expect the men of the church to rally to us."

And they did. Bedding was put in the back of the church. The Ladies Working Society furnished food to those volunteering their services and from time to time cooked cakes and other desserts. Many grocery items were donated. When the weather was good, church members built a fire in the yard, around which they sang and talked. People on the island who had never been to church came to participate. All experienced a twinge of sorrow when the fence was finally installed.

The same generosity of spirit was in evidence when it came

time to seal the church's roof. The women raised money for the material, and the men camped in the churchyard and worked for free.

"Oh, it was lovely, wonderful, and a great privilege to work in those dark days among those dear people," said Mrs. Legare. "All went to church in carts and wagons, and how!"

When the church needed carpet, those who had sheep gave wool generously. Those who had no sheep sent money. All the members helped at carpet making, and in a short while, the carpet was down.

"When cyclones and earthquakes wrecked the property, not once did those faithful hearts falter in their allegiance to their precious Zion," concluded Mrs. Legare.

Johns Island is alternately known as Fenwick Island in recognition

Johns Island Presbyterian Church

of Fenwick Hall, the most imposing residence on the island for over two hundred years now. The mansion stands on the old Indian trails near the banks of the lovely Stono River, its gardens and grounds set in the pine forests.

In 1730, John Fenwick—the seventh man by that name in his line—replaced the log house used for a dwelling since before 1717 with a two-story brick residence on a strong basement. It was constructed as a fort. From the cellar, an underground passageway ran to a creek connected to the Stono River. The interior walls of the house were paneled, and the mantelpieces were carved in classical designs. On the roof was an observation platform.

The Fenwick property was the setting for one of the most tragic romances in South Carolina history.

The chief business at Fenwick Hall was the raising of racehorses at the famous stables. The best young bloods of the region came on their thoroughbreds to woo Sir Edward Fenwick's lovely daughters.

But one of the fairest of the daughters committed the unforgivable sin of falling in love with her father's head groom. After eloping on one of Sir Edward's swiftest thoroughbreds, they were delayed at Stono Ferry, where they were overtaken by members of the family, headed by the girl's enraged father. Then and there, her husband-to-be was tried by a mock court and convicted as a horse thief. The girl's supplications were disregarded, and the young man was hanged upon an oak tree before her eyes. Her mind never recovered from the shock, and tradition says her spirit still walks the grounds.

After the last of the Fenwicks moved away from the area, the old hall stood empty, listening to the whispering of the pines and the cry of seabirds, for no caretaker would live there. Johns Island old-timers say that a curse was put on the place. From the tall tower to the basement, footsteps are heard, and the dark waters of a hidden well sometimes reflect a lovely face. "When first dark comes, the spirit walks under the oaks by Stono Ferry, wringing its hands," local people say. On dark nights, the sound of racing hooves is heard on King's Highway. When the moon shines, a proud lady in misty white glides by the side of her lover in the shadows under the oak trees.

Johns Island saw its share of action during the Revolutionary War.

A company of colonials was stationed on the island in 1778. General Augustine Prevost, in command of the British, was encamped on the opposite side of the Stono River at Stono Ferry. Thomas Fenwick of Johns Island came into the camp of the colonials, supped with the officers, and gained information, which he passed to the British. Acting on Fenwick's information, two divisions of British soldiers crossed the river at night. The colonial quarters were surrounded and every man made a prisoner. A company under Colonel Robert Barnwell surrendered to a British sergeant who promised honorable treatment but actually began a bayonet attack that killed most of Barnwell's men.

In another Revolutionary War battle on Johns Island, at Wappoo Cut, the Americans routed the British but could not maintain their advantage because reinforcements were delayed by low tide.

As with South Carolina's other sea islands, Johns Island's plantation economy was heavily dependent on the labor of slaves. The following story—related by Mike Lawrence, who worked on one of the island's plantations—tells of a time when one slave out-witted and got the upper hand on his master.

When the Major gave a dance, he always call upon Old John Drayton, the smartest man who work on the Major's place. What been more, Old John play for all the dances on the plantation. He made his fiddle talk. When Massa give dance, he always call 'pon John.

One day, the Major send word to John that the cow done break out of the pasture, and he got to mend the fence quick. But John done promise to play for a dance. And he steal down the path and go.

The Major ask everybody where John, and the people all band together and tell him they see John leave in the boat to go fish and they think John might be drown. The Major engage four men to shoot gun over creek to make John's body rise. The Major gone to bed with heavy heart 'cause he been very fond of John.

John come back and before day he go to work on fence rail. Now, one hundred rail been called a good day's work, but Old John decide he's going to do better than that. He found five trees growing close together, and he cut piece out of every one. Then he chop at the biggest tree till he fall, and that tree knock all the rest over with 'um. When dem tree fall together, it make such a noise, the Major hear 'um in his bed, and he hasten to dress so he can see what going on.

When he see Old John cutting away, he been sure enough glad to see John ain't drown. He start to say something, but Old John say, "Go away. I ain't got time to talk with you now."

The Major go home, and when he go back to the woods,
he see that Old John done cut five hundred rails that day.

The slave descendants who remain on Johns Island are said to have retained some of the superstitions—and some of the inexplicable powers—for which their ancestors were noted. One local story concerns a grieving woman who, while attending the funeral of her only child, called out, "The three boys who killed my Esau will not go free, and the law don't have to do nothing!" As the mourners looked on, she "dressed the coffin" in her individual way, covering it with strange items and chanting unintelligible threats. The boy was finally laid to rest, and nothing was thought of the mother's pledge. That is, until three weeks later, when two of the boys believed to have killed her son lost their lives in an automobile accident and the third was found dead in his bed.

One of the most popular tourist sites on the island easily predates slave days, British colonization, Columbus's discovery of America, and even recorded Indian habitation. The Angel Oak stands 65 feet tall, has a circumference of 25½ feet, and shades a 17,000-square-foot area. The length of its largest limb is 89 feet. The oak is reported to be in excess of 1,400 years old.

The property on which it stands was part of a land grant received by Abraham Waight in 1717. Waight was a prosperous planter who owned several plantations, including The Point, where the Angel Oak stood. The property later passed to Martha Waight Angel and Justis Angel, who acquired it in 1810. Members of the Angel family are buried near the oak in the cemetery of St. Johns Episcopal Church.

Angel Oak

The Magnolia Garden Club cared for the tree and grounds until the late 1970s. The city of Charleston acquired the Angel Oak and its surrounding property in 1991. Angel Oak Park is now open to the public. There is no admission charge.

Johns Island retains its ghostly heritage even today. Mary Roper Richardson told of an experience she had while working in the gift shop at Angel Oak Park in October 1991:

> It was a dreadful day, dark and dreary. I just strolled around the gift shop, having nothing to do. Suddenly, I noticed a woman coming in by the back door. I had not heard a car, nor had I noticed any person in the vicinity. The woman was white, very pale, and she was dressed in black—black coat,

black shoes. She smiled and asked me if I enjoyed working here. I told her I enjoyed it very much. But I was quite surprised by her next question. She asked me if I was afraid to work in such a remote place on the island. Then she looked at me and said, "You don't ever have to be afraid to work here. There is always someone watching out for you."

She left by the front door as quickly as she had arrived by the back. I heard no car, and I don't know where she went. I asked other employees if they had ever seen her, and they said they had not. But I want you to know that I have had a contented feeling since that day, and I've never been afraid, even on dark days when we have no customers.

There are stark symbols of urban sprawl on the island today. Johns Island is shrugging off some of the old ways. Baptisms are no longer conducted in the river, where the preacher dipped white-robed candidates into the briny ebb tide, the best tide for washing away sins. And it is becoming difficult to find anyone who speaks pure Gullah, the haunting dialect that belonged only to South Carolina's sea islands and coastal districts.

Still, many traces of earlier times remain. Visitors cannot help being captivated by Fenwick Hall, which stands majestically at the end of its avenue of oaks; Johns Island Presbyterian Church, virtuous in its old age; the Angel Oak, more ancient than the area's human history; and the island's ghosts, new and old.

Charleston Tea Plantation

One of the main attractions on Wadmalaw Island is Charleston Tea Plantation, the only tea farm in America.

In 1799, French botanist André Michaux planted the first tea ever cultivated in America at nearby Middleton Place Gardens. Much later, Dr. Charles Shepherd, a biochemist at the Medical College of South Carolina, grew tea successfully for twenty-seven years at Pinehurst Tea Farm, near Summerville. The Lipton company evaluated some tea shrubs growing at Pinehurst Tea Farm and decided to transfer them to a former potato farm on Wadmalaw.

With its humid weather, Wadmalaw proved fitting for the cultivation of tea. Tea horticulturist Mack Fleming directed a Lipton research facility on the island prior to joining with William Barclay Hall to form Charleston Tea Plantation, Inc., in 1987. Hall is a third-generation English-trained tea taster who assures the highest quality from each day's harvest. He speaks to groups in the area about his London apprenticeship, during which he sampled eight hundred to a thousand cups a day, five days a week. His presentation draws a laugh a second. He says there are few women tea tasters because women find it hard to spit in public a thousand times a day.

American Classic Tea is harvested by a one-of-a-kind machine, designed on the premises, that performs as well as the hand labor utilized in other countries. The tea operation employs people from Wadmalaw and other rural areas near Charleston, providing needed jobs in the area.

Shoppers can find American Classic Tea—the official "Hospitality Beverage" of South Carolina—on grocery-store shelves everywhere. Its producers consider it the freshest tea available and are proud that it is grown without the use of insecticides or fungicides, for a cleaner, purer tea than imports.

Wadmalaw Island's history goes back more than 130 years before André Michaux ever thought of cultivating tea in the New World. Robert Sandford and his party explored the island in 1666, a year before the settlement of Charles Town. In the name of the king of England and the Lords Proprietors, Sandford laid claim to Carolina westward from the Atlantic Ocean to the "Southern Seas." On Wadmalaw, he met the friendly Indian tribes ruled by the Cassique of Kiawah.

On December 20, 1771, Benjamin Jenkins purchased a Wadmalaw Island plantation known as "The Rocks" from Thomas Tucker. Its 496 acres included a small island in the marsh. Jenkins was a member of the provincial assembly from the parish of St. John's Colleton. In his will of May 10, 1781, he bequeathed The Rocks to his two sons, Benjamin and Samuel.

The plantation's marsh island became a summer resort for Wadmalaw planters who wanted to be close to the sea when the hot months came. The church and the whitewashed cottages with wraparound porches, all built around a square, were the essence of a cool, picturesque place.

Like other South Carolina barrier islands, Wadmalaw was later recognized for its superior sea-island cotton. The rules, restrictions, and punishments for the island's field hands were as varied as the planters themselves. Prince Smith, once a slave on Wadmalaw Island, gave the following account to Augustus Ladson of Charleston:

> Slaves on other plantations had to hide from their master to have meeting. We could have ours any night we want to even without his consent. When Master went to town, any slave could ask him to buy things for them in Charleston.
>
> He had about four hundred acres of land which he divided in two halves by a fence. He would plant one side and let cattle graze on the other. . . . A whole hand, or a slave in his

prime, was given two tasks for his day's work. A task carried from twenty-four to twenty-five rows, which was thirty-five feet long. A three-fourths hand was given twelve rows. An old slave was called a half-hand, and they did half an acre a day. When it was time to pick the cotton, the three-fourths hand had to pick thirty pounds, and the half-hand had twenty-four for a day's work.

Master had three kind o' punishment for those who disobeyed him. One was the sweat box. That was made the height of the person and no larger. You were squeezed in and the box nailed. In summer, it was put in the hot sun, and in the winter, it was in the coldest and dampest place. The next was the stock. The person lying on the floor with foots tied to a heavy weight. The third was the Bilbo. You placed on a high scaffold for so many hours and you try to keep a level head or you fall and you surely break your neck.

When Fort Sumter fired on, Master carry seventy of us to Greenville on account of its mountains. He believe mountains protect from Yankees. One Tuesday morning, bright and early, Sherman came into Greenville on a horse and order everybody to surrender. We stayed there until harvesting time.

After the Civil War, the postcard-perfect town of Rockville, located a mile past Charleston Tea Plantation at land's end, became the site of the first sailing regattas in South Carolina. The Rockville Races, organized in 1890 by the planters of Wadmalaw Island, Edisto Island, and the neighboring islands, drew large crowds.

The first race, now woven into local legend, was inspired—or instigated—by the Reverend B. B. Sams. When Sams left

Rockville Yacht Club

Beaufort to begin preaching in Rockville, he brought along his sailboat, the *Marguerite*. The sight of the clergyman sailing the waters of Bohicket Creek and the North Edisto aroused feelings of rivalry in James Island yachtsmen. Shortly thereafter, the "Jim Island boys," led by W. Reynolds Jenkins, sailed the first race against the Rockville preacher.

Soon, other yacht clubs began to enter the annual event. Old-timers still laugh as they tell the story of the 1908 regatta, when the Carolina Yacht Club's entry, racing in Rockville for the first time, capsized, throwing Arthur Young, Alex Marshall, Judge William H. Grimball, and William H. Haskell into the waters of the North Edisto.

Today, visitors come from near and far to watch the three-day Sea Island Regatta in August. After each exciting day of racing comes an evening dance at the yacht club, with music provided by an orchestra from Charleston. Few occasions are as much fun for both islanders and inland spectators.

Hidden by live oaks draped with gray moss, Rockville doesn't come into view until one is actually in the village. The town may reach its height of beauty during regatta week, but visitors will readily testify that any day is a great day to visit Rockville.

When driving the island's roads today, visitors will not see any houses except those of slave descendants, and they might think Wadmalaw otherwise uninhabited. However, the little, unassuming roads that branch off from the main road here and there lead eventually to rambling plantation houses, holdovers from the days

Old store in Rockville

of sea-island cotton. Most of the homes sit precariously near the water's edge.

There is one notable exception to these locally built mansions. Around 1970, T. Ladson Webb, a Charleston insurance executive, bought a Johns Island home and floated it thirty-five miles to Wadmalaw. The voyage of the eighty-ton antebellum house was only part of the story. Just moving the structure across Johns Island involved crossing twenty-six ditches, some of them twelve feet wide. Webb had a massive slip dug into the riverside to allow the entry of the heavy-duty barge that would tote the home down the Stono River into the Intracoastal Waterway. The barge then deposited the structure on the bank at Webb's summer home-site on Wadmalaw, where his former house had burned. It took ten weeks from the start of the project until the house was finally perched sixty feet inland from the bank of Bohicket Creek. It remains there today.

KIAWAH ISLAND

Kiawah scene

𝒦*iawah* 𝒥*sland*, eleven miles long and three miles across at its widest point, was likely discovered in June 1666 when Robert Sandford, "secretary and chief register for the right honorable Lords Proprietors of their County Clarendon, Province of Carolina," was sent on a voyage of discovery.

When Sandford arrived at the Edisto River, he didn't know

exactly where he was. He sailed about four miles up the river and anchored. A canoe bearing two Indians promptly appeared. They came aboard and responded willingly to Sandford's questions—though in what language he does not tell. Before departing, the Indians invited him to come to their principal town to trade.

The next day, Sandford and a party from his "vessell" entered "a creek on the east shore, a very fair and deep creek or river going north and easterly, being gone about a mile to Bohicket Creek." The site, near the Bohicket Indian village, was located about where the town of Rockville on Wadmalaw Island is today.

Here, in the presence of the ship's company, Sandford declared formal possession by "turff and twigg" of the whole country "from Lat. 36 degrees North to 29 degrees South, and West to the Southern Seas, by name of the Province of Carolina for our Sovereign Lord, Charles II, King of England, and the Right Honorable Lords Proprietors."

The next day, Sandford and his men sailed to the chief Indian village. A large party of Indians awaited them at the landing. Among these was a "Captain of the Nation" named Shadee—the man known as the Cassique (or Chief) of Kiawah. He invited the company to spend the night at his town, a short distance away. Since Sandford wanted to know the "forms, manner and populousness" of the place—as well as the power of the Cassique—he permitted four of his company to go. They returned the next morning highly pleased with the way they had been entertained, the goodness of the land, and the beautiful town itself.

The name *Kiawah* once applied to the area of Charles Town Landing, which Sandford referred to as "the country of Kyawha."

Apparently, it also applied to the Indian tribe, its principal village, and the river, which Sandford renamed the Ashley. Through the years, the name has known many spellings: Key-war, Keyawah, Kyawaw, Kayawah, Chyawhaw, Keawa, Kiwaha, Kywaha, Keywaha, and Kiawah, now the accepted form.

"That island lying between ye Mouth of Stonoe River and North Edistoe, commonly Known by ye Name of Kiawah island" was granted to Captain George Raynor in 1699, shortly after the Kiawah Indians gave up all claims to the land to the king of England in exchange for beads and hatchets. Raynor's daughter, Mary, inherited the property. In 1717, after her death, half of Kiawah was acquired by John Stanyarne, a planter. A short time before his death in 1772, Stanyarne built a plantation house which remains on Kiawah today, although in a decayed condition.

Stanyarne left the Kiawah property to his granddaughters, Mary Gibbes and Elizabeth Raven Vanderhorst. Elizabeth was the wife of Arnoldus Vanderhorst, who acquired title to most of the island. Stanyarne's house eventually came to be known by Vanderhorst's name.

The Van der Horsts, as they were called in the early years, were likely among the Knickerbocker settlers of New York, many of whom moved to the Charles Town vicinity around 1761. Captain Arnoldus Van der Horst was a son of Major John Van der Horst. He served in the Revolutionary War and was elected a member of the Society of Cincinnati in 1806. His son Arnoldus Vanderhorst, who acquired the courtesy title of "General," was a militia captain and a member of the American legislature during the Revolutionary War. He was intendant (mayor) of Charleston when President George Washington visited the city in 1791 and

The Vanderhorst Mansion today

was governor of South Carolina from 1794 to 1796. He was an active Federalist and therefore a conservative. Yet as governor, he urged the legislature to revise the state's criminal code, which he termed "gothic." He was also a passionate agriculturist and hunter.

The Vanderhorsts' wealth came from growing indigo, but they later expanded into sea-island cotton. Cotton was grown on the island until the coming of the boll weevil around 1919.

Union troops occupied the Vanderhorst Mansion during the Civil War. Some of them even left their signatures on an attic dormer, along with a greeting for the Confederate commander who had ordered the firing on Fort Sumter: "How are you this morning, General Beauregard?"

A ghost tale is told of the four-story mansion.

Arnoldus Vanderhorst was fond of hosting hunting parties, for which he issued invitations to plantation masters on other islands as well as on the mainland. A man called Squash was in charge of delivering the invitations and directing the hunts.

During one hunt, as Squash was preparing lunch, General Vanderhorst wandered away, carrying his gun. A shot was heard. When his master failed to return, Squash went in search of him. He found Vanderhorst in a ditch where he had fallen and fatally shot himself.

Squash was a broken man. For as long as he lived, he sat on the porch of the Vanderhorst Mansion and told hunting stories to anyone who would listen. It is believed that even today, visitors to the mansion can sometimes hear the voice of Squash telling the old hunting stories.

In 1934, when he was doing research for *Porgy and Bess*, George Gershwin attended a prayer meeting at a small church on Kiawah Island whose members were descendants of the Vanderhorst slaves. Gershwin sat in a pew at the back of the church to listen to the compelling prayers and watch the worshipers beat a complicated pattern with hands and feet. He called the island Kittewah in his famous folk opera.

Kiawah remained in the Vanderhorst family until 1950, when it was bought by C. C. Royal, a wealthy lumberman, for $125,000. In 1952, a causeway and bridge were built to connect Kiawah with Johns Island.

Wild goats and pigs, the descendants of livestock raised nearly two hundred years earlier on the plantation of Arnoldus Vanderhorst, were still roaming the dense palmetto marshes early in 1974 when the Kuwait Investment Company—half-owned by the Kuwaiti government and half by private Arab investors—paid the heirs of C. C. Royal $17.4 million for the bulk of the island. The Kuwaitis' purchase included everything but a small subdivision of peeling summer houses and the year-round residence of Eugenia Mae Royal, C. C. Royal's widow. The new owners planned to invest up to $225 million to make the island into a first-class resort community, with hotels, houses, and recreational facilities.

Then the rumors started. Some said the Arabs were stockpiling artillery on Kiawah.

And then the Kuwaitis were informed that their eleven miles of unspoiled Atlantic beach comprised one of the last nesting grounds of the loggerhead turtle. Loggerheads favored Kiawah mostly because its beaches were dark at night. The turtles were so large that whole families sometimes stood on the back of a single loggerhead for a photograph session. Cooperating with environmentalists, the Kuwaitis ensured that no light would reach the beach at night. Turtle protection didn't come cheaply; the owners spent about twenty thousand dollars a year for it.

Next, the talk turned to preserving the island as a national seashore. Proponents began circulating petitions. The Kuwaitis were distressed when the dispute was covered by the *Washington Post*, the *New York Times*, and CBS.

In 1988, Kiawah Resort Associates, a joint venture group, bought the property from the Kuwaitis for $105 million, the most expensive real-estate transaction in South Carolina history. Charleston businessman Charles S. Way, Jr., was the principal architect of the purchase.

Today, Kiawah Island is best known as a world-class golf resort. Tennis and beachcombing are also available to those who rent a room in the upscale hotel or one of the villas. Though development on the island has been of high quality, there seems to be no plan for preservation and restoration of the historic plantation manor house. Perhaps that will lie in the future, for Kiawah has indeed known many changes.

YONGES ISLAND

The original town on Yonges Island was first called London and then New London before becoming known as Wiltown around 1697. The name is believed to honor William I, prince of Orange (1533–84), the father of the Dutch republic. He was called "William the Silent" because of his cautious nature.

One early account suggests there were more than two dozen houses in Wiltown, which was protected by a small fort. The village was attacked by the Yemassee Indians in July 1715. After the Indians were turned away, the fort was used as a base for boats patrolling the area.

The name Wiltown was eventually corrupted to Willtown. Most of the early settlers were Presbyterians. The Reverend Archibald Stono, who founded Johns Island Presbyterian Church, preached at the meeting house built on Yonges.

On one occasion, word came of a slave rebellion. The Presbyterians, many of whom were militiamen, were called to arms. They apprehended the slaves. When the followers saw that their leaders were to be executed, they quickly scattered, and that was the end of the insurrection.

For the next century, Willtown was controlled by the Elliott family. William Elliott, a Charles Town planter, was granted twenty-four lots in the village. After his death, his daughter Ann and her husband, Lewis Morris, came into possession of the Willtown lots and other land in the area. Their home was called Oaklodge.

Ann and Lewis Morris had a son, also named Lewis, who married Elizabeth Manigault of Charleston. The bride's father, Gabriel Manigault, is credited with the arrival of the Federal style in South Carolina.

In 1809, Lewis and Elizabeth built a house at Willtown Bluff overlooking the Edisto River and the village. During sixteen years of marriage, the Morrises had nine children, one of them born on a ship en route from Charleston to New York. Elizabeth died in a hurricane in 1822 when a house at Sullivan's Island crashed down on her. Later, when Lewis announced his engagement to marry Amarinthia Lowndes, his children were "inexpressibly astonished," according to a friend. The children of the second marriage did not survive to maturity.

In 1852, lots at Willtown Bluff were selling for an average of twenty-six dollars. But the area's prosperity was shattered by the Civil War. Confederate forces fortified the bluff. On one occasion, two field artillery pieces drove back a Union party approaching by the river.

Everyone worried about an attack, and with good reason. Before daybreak one morning, the transport *Enoch Dean* and two smaller Union boats, the *Milton* and the *John Adams*, stole into the area under cover of a heavy fog. Although the three-gun battery at Willtown Bluff fired, the boats made landfall. Lewis Morris's rice mill, his stores of rice, his canal gates, and his bales of fine sea-island cotton were destroyed.

Morris died at the age of seventy-eight on October 4, 1863. The Morris Plantation manor house survived, but some other prominent Willtown Bluff homes, such as the original house at Prospect Hill Plantation, were burned.

Lewis Morris's plantation went through several owners before

Willtown Bluff on the Edisto River

it was purchased by Christopher FitzSimons in 1911. His wife was to discover that the manor house was haunted.

Upon hearing a strange noise one evening, Mrs. FitzSimons got up to check on her children. Finding them snug in their beds, she returned to her room. "As I opened my door to enter," she remembered, "I saw standing behind a large easy chair an old woman, a stranger to me. Only for an instant did I see her."

On another occasion, as Mrs. FitzSimons entered the dining room, she discovered "a house servant of the old regime, as simply dressed as a quakeress and immaculate in her tight-waisted calico dress with its full skirt. She moved with purpose at an accustomed duty."

Once, as Mrs. FitzSimons was folding laundry, she gazed up and saw a statuesque woman with a pleasant expression on her face. She was to remember the sighting for the rest of her life. "I think of her as Agnes," she said. "For many a stately Agnes like her had I seen in the old days."

Mrs. FitzSimons was never frightened of the ghosts she so frequently beheld. "I feel no awe of the mysteries as I sit alone in the night . . . or of the old house which has become a part of me and my life," she once remarked.

The lovely Willtown Bluff house still stands overlooking a curve of the Edisto River.

The second Prospect Hill manor house sits at the end of an avenue of oaks. Prospect Hill Plantation was owned by William H. Manigault, who died intestate in 1858 after an accidental fall from a third-floor window of a New York hotel. The plantation then came into the hands of Edward and Margaret Manigault Barnwell, who had married in 1835 and eventually became the parents of seventeen children. In 1859, Edward Barnwell produced over a million pounds of rice with the help of 245 slaves. Margaret died in 1864 at age forty-four. In 1865, Edward watched as Union troops burned his plantation home. He died in 1885.

A relative, Stephen Elliott Barnwell, then bought Prospect Hill. In 1890, he leased an acre of land to local African-Americans for the construction of Bethlehem A.M.E. Church. The lease was to last ninety-nine years at a rate of one cent a year.

Stephen Barnwell lost Prospect Hill for debt. Title to the property changed hands several times before 1927, when E. F. Hutton bought the land. He conveyed Prospect Hill Plantation to his brother, Franklyn L. Hutton, on October 31, 1929.

Many members of the famous group known as "the Four Hundred"—the four hundred people of highest society, as reckoned by Mrs. William Backhouse Astor, Jr., and her collaborator, Ward McAllister—came to the coast of South Carolina during the 1930s and acquired plantations for use as hunting preserves. Franklyn L. Hutton, retired New York stockbroker, was one of them. What he erected on Yonges Island was nothing less than a little kingdom.

The second Prospect Hill manor house was occupied by Joseph Ruffra, superintendent of the plantation, who had charge of protecting and feeding game, caring for and breeding horses, and maintaining the estate in general. Hutton built a hunting lodge for himself and his family on what had been Oakhurst Plantation.

He named his lodge Curley Hut, after his second wife, the former Irene Curley. The second floor of the house had four guest bedrooms, bedrooms for Mr. and Mrs. Hutton, and Mr. Hutton's den. Downstairs were a sun parlor, a game room with a billiard

Prospect Hill

table and other equipment, a gun room with a bar, a living room, and a dining room. But the most outstanding room on the first floor was the office, called "the Zebra Room" because the furniture was upholstered with zebra skins. Its walls were paneled in walnut from trees cut on the place.

Hutton had a great love for the Low Country. He came early in November and remained as late as May. When the hunting season ended in South Carolina, he went to Czechoslovakia for more. He had a house at Palm Beach and an apartment in New York for use when no hunting was to be had.

He built an elaborate shooting range on Yonges in which twenty-six clay-pigeon traps were hidden behind shrubbery. As one walked along, each of the traps was sprung in turn, so that the clay pigeons came whizzing from unexpected angles. The hunter who broke sixteen of the twenty-six was considered a good shot. Two of the traps fired straight at the sportsman.

One of Hutton's favorite hobbies was raising horses. He had about thirty, including an Arabian stallion and some Fahl ponies from Scotland. He crossbred the Fahl ponies with native marsh tackies. He also experimented with raising chukars, an East Indian game bird resembling a partridge.

There is a tale that daughter Barbara, known as "the richest girl in the world," fell in love with the man in charge of the horses.

The story of Barbara Hutton, possibly the most famous heiress in the world, began in Hollywood, where she was born in 1912. She was the daughter of Franklyn L. Hutton and Edna Woolworth, one of three daughters of the founder of the great five-and-dime chain. At four, she saw her mother die. Her grandfather, with whom she spent much time, died when she was seven and her grandmother when she was twelve. "My father was young and very busy," she once said. "He loved me, of course, but I was only an ordinary, rather stupid little girl and I couldn't be a real companion to a gay, brilliant young man, could I?"

When her father refused to allow her to wed the man she loved, she married Prince Alexis Mdivani, a nobleman from Soviet Georgia. Mdivani scolded Barbara for being fat and put her on a strict diet, which she continued until the end of her life. Some of her relatives believed Mdivani's actions impaired her health. After divorcing the prince, she married Count Haugwitz-Reventlow, then others, including movie star Cary Grant. Old-time islanders believe Barbara Hutton would have had a much happier life had she been permitted to marry the man of her choice.

The Huttons traveled to South Carolina in their private railroad car. Although Charleston aristocrats didn't accept wealthy Northerners into their society, the Huttons had family in the vicinity. E. F. Hutton owned Laurel Spring Plantation on the Combahee River.

The family's dog kennels on Yonges were so elaborate that they once caused an altercation between a newspaper reporter and the islanders.

Chlotilde R. Martin of Beaufort spent weeks working on an article about the Huttons. During her research, she was cordially received into the homes of many islanders, where she found warmth, courtesy, and delicious food. Without exception, the islanders remarked that the Huttons' kennels were finer than any they had ever dreamed of.

The article that appeared in the newspaper revealed that each dog lived in a two-room suite with a bed built off the floor and its own private dishes for food. What the islanders objected to was Martin's description of them as Hutton's "simple Low Country neighbors, and their goggle-eyed interest in his handsome dog kennels."

"None of these people could believe it when they heard that such a fine house had been built for dogs, so the entire countryside went to see for itself," Martin wrote. "And it still gets goggle-eyed when it talks about those dog kennels."

Martin later printed an apology.

In December 1940, Curley Hut was the scene of Franklyn L. Hutton's funeral. In March 1943, Prospect Hill was sold for $112,500 to M. L. McLeod and others. The new owners were chiefly interested in the timber on the place. McLeod's company eventually held title to twenty-two former rice plantations. Under its ownership, Prospect Hill again became a working plantation. Some of the descendants of Willtown slaves came to work there. The new owners bought a combine to help in harvesting the rice crop.

In December 1952, a portion of the Hutton property was sold to G. Herman Dryer and his wife, Eileen. In later years, Curley Hut was neglected. A circle of cats could be seen gobbling food from a dishpan on the front porch. In September 1987, the thirty-five-room house burned. Firefighters battled the blaze for sixteen hours. Mrs. Dryer was rescued from a second-story room. Only two chimneys and portions of two rooms were left in the aftermath.

Although Prospect Hill Plantation was the scene of many high-society functions, the rest of Yonges Island was primarily agrarian. A few farmers were still planting sea-island cotton after the turn of the twentieth century. Before long, the oyster and shrimp industry began taking over as a means of making a living for many island families.

L. P. Maggioni, who installed oyster-canning factories on Daufuskie and other islands, established one on Yonges. The plant operated seven months of the year. From October to the first of May, oysters were gathered from the salty creek beds and river bottoms leased to the company by the state of South Carolina. Flatboats manned by sturdy islanders covered a wide territory including Wadmalaw Sound, the South Edisto River, and its tributaries. The oysters were gathered at dead low water, and the vessels would return to the docks with gunwales almost awash. Oarsmen stood in the stern propelling the craft with long paddles in the manner of Venetian gondoliers. Oysters were canned by local labor at the factory and shipped to Savannah for distribution.

Reports filed with the state board of fisheries showed that 127,706 bushels of oysters were handled at the Yonges Island plant in 1938. The odor of shrimp and fish pervaded the island. Mustard-colored dwellings and warehouses huddled together on the little promontory that rose up from the salt marshes. Freight boats tied up to the same wharf where sea-island cotton was once unloaded. The talk of longshoremen and the clatter and bang of machinery echoed up and down the river.

Today, Yonges Island remains a delightful place to visit. It may seem unusual that such a remote island was so deeply appealing to wealthy people, but visitors today can verify it with their own eyes. The second Prospect Hill manor house, constructed by the Barnwell family in 1876, is now owned by Richard M. Holtzman, who raises American Paint horses. And the Morris Plantation manor house, which overlooks the Edisto River, is still visible at the end of a scenic road.

EDISTO ISLAND

Edisto Island is one of the oldest settlements in South Carolina. Once the home of the Edistow Indians, it still bears traces of their presence. There is a shell mound of Indian origin on the beach that many people believe to be an ancient ceremonial site.

The first white men to set foot on Edisto were probably priests who belonged to the Spanish colony in Florida. It appears that Father Rogel, a Jesuit, was sent to establish a mission on Orista (the Spanish name for Edisto) in August 1569. His mission was located near the banks of the South Edisto River.

Father Rogel must have spent considerable time with the Indians, for it is recorded that he preached to them in their own language. He failed, however, to make much of an impression on them. They didn't like his doctrine because, as they put it, "he spoke evil about the devil." They finally refused to listen to him, and his work went largely for naught.

William Hilton, commanding the ship *Adventure*, sighted the lands watered by the Edisto River in 1663 but lacked the opportunity to explore them. He reported that the Edisto was "a fair and goodly river, branching out into several branches and bays, and deep, and is fresh water within 2 leagues of the mouth." Indians met the men of the expedition and gave them "a great store of fish, large Mullets, young Basse, Shads, and several other sorts of very good and well tasted fish." Hilton's men saw deer, turkeys, and partridges in abundance and were much impressed by the richness of the island.

It was in 1674 that the Earl of Shaftesbury purchased the island from the Edistow Indians. Land grants were soon issued. Although the English colonists must have realized they were risking enemy attack by settling along the river shores of Edisto Island, they were willing to take their chances, since an excellent living could be made in agriculture or by trading with the Indians.

In 1686, the Spanish attacked suddenly with three ships, a hundred white men, and an auxiliary force of Indians and slaves. They sacked the houses of the colonists, including that of Paul Grimball, the holder of a grant of six hundred acres along the North Edisto River. The Grimballs returned from Charles Town to find their plantation in shambles. No murders were committed on Edisto, but Kitts Oats, an English maid, was "carried away captif and [the Spanish] keeps her," according to an eyewitness.

Clergyman, soldier, and scholar William Dunlop wrote an

account "of losses and damages by the Spanyds who came from Saint Augustine August 1686." According to Dunlop, the invaders "staid at his [Paul Grimball's] house and lands, wasting, robbing and killing and destroying said Grimball's horses and catell." He noted the loss of "several tabell clos, household lining, two lamps, fine wearing apparall for women and children and servant" and the destruction of "200 traces of choice onions, tobacco green in the field, and 100 large hoggs."

By 1694, farmers were living and working on the island. Some planters tried cultivating rice, but that venture was soon abandoned due to the water's unsuitable salinity. But all was not lost. Once indigo cultivation began, it brought fortunes to the island planters, as England held out a handsome bounty for its production. Indigo was planted on the island even after the Revolutionary War, until about the 1820s. However, it was the long-staple cotton introduced in 1790 that brought the planters their greatest prosperity.

Edisto Island became famous for its superb grade of sea-island cotton. It has been written that Edisto cotton didn't go to market because French lace mills contracted for it before the seed was planted. The finest cotton on the island was grown by men like John F. Townsend, J. Mason Seabrook, Isaac Jenkins Mikell, and Ephraim Clark, who treasured their particular strains and jealously guarded their secrets, handing them down from father to son. The enormous prices realized by the planters resulted in some of the largest fortunes in the early history of the state. The planters built comfortable manor houses on the island and magnificent mansions in Charleston, where they enjoyed the sophistication of antebellum society.

Some of the island's plantations and their owners are legendary.

Ephraim Mikell Baynard made his fortune growing sea-island cotton on Little Edisto, Seaside, LaRoche, and Rabbit Point Plantations, all on Edisto. He employed 370 slaves in 1860. By that time, he had come to be known as South Carolina's first millionaire. Baynard remained a bachelor, having been engaged to a woman who died before the wedding took place. He had spent a considerable amount of money on the expected wedding, including taking a trip to New York to buy furniture and housewares. But after the death of his fiancée, he lived so conservatively that his friends nicknamed him "the Miser." That judgment was proven premature when he contributed $166,000 to the College of Charleston in 1864.

Isaac Jenkins Mikell lived at Peter's Point, the manor house that many consider the most stunning on the island. The house is still in existence but is a far cry from what it was during the heyday

Old cemetery at Peter's Point

of sea-island cotton production. Like many of the old island homes, it had a wide hall running straight through to the back, high ceilings, large windows, and superior ventilation. The architectural style owed much to the tradition of the West Indies, where catching the breezes was an essential consideration in home construction. The Peter's Point grounds bordered St. Pierre Creek, which flows into the South Edisto River. The house overlooks St. Helena Sound, one of the noblest seascapes of the area.

Mikell also owned a house at 94 Rutledge Avenue in Charleston, one of the finest homes in the city at that time. The social and cultural life of the city drew the planters during the winter months, when work on the plantations was slack and activities in Charleston were at their gayest and most stimulating. Planter fami-

Mikell House in Charleston

Isaac Jenkins Mikell monument

lies attended balls and the theater and mingled with notable politicians and intellectuals.

In addition to Peter's Point and his Charleston mansion, Mikell owned two other sea-island cotton plantations. The Peter's Point house later passed to Isaac Jenkins Mikell, Jr., the author of *Rumbling of the Chariot Wheels* (1923), a boyhood reminiscence of life on a Southern plantation before and during the Civil War.

Another Edisto plantation that was testimony to the fortunes made there was Brick House, built between 1720 and 1725 by Paul Hamilton, the grandfather of Paul Hamilton III, who was elected governor of South Carolina and appointed secretary of the navy under President James Madison. The brick for the house was obtained in Boston, where a finer and sturdier quality was produced than plantation-made brick. Salt-free sand and gravel were hauled from the mainland. Timber was cut on another of Hamilton's plantations; all the lumber used in construction was seasoned for seven years. The floor joists were of oak.

Brick House

The high-pitched roof soared over rooms filled with paintings. The many stucco enrichments gave the mansion the air of a French home of the time of Henry IV or Louis XIII.

In 1798, Brick House passed into the hands of the Jenkins family. Benjamin Jenkins was a member of the Council of Safety and had been an officer in the Collection Regiment during the Revolutionary War. Colonel Joseph Jenkins of Brick House was an Edisto Island delegate to the Secession Convention before the Civil War.

William Seabrook built the home known as the Old Seabrook Mansion sometime after 1810 and etched his initials in the ironwork on the entrance stairs. Seabrook was one of the most prosperous planters on all of South Carolina's sea islands. Born on Edisto in 1773, he overcame the financial reverses that followed the Revolutionary War. At the age of seventeen, he became man-

ager of his and his mother's estates. He was one of the first planters to produce sea-island cotton, and he experimented with the
use of salt for fertilizer for his fields. He also established a steam-
boat line between Savannah and Charleston, with stops at all the
islands along the route.

The house had a two-story portico and was built in a design
popular in Charleston. It became a prototype for other houses,
particularly Seabrook's son's home at Oak Island and Isaac Jenkins
Mikell's family seat at Peter's Point. The style of the Old Seabrook
Mansion has been compared to that of James Hoban, architect of
the White House, who worked in Charleston for a short time
during the 1790s.

The Seabrook family owned more than a thousand slaves. Doz-
ens of slave children were assigned the task of picking up leaves
as they fell from the trees in order to maintain the mansion's
lawn in perfect condition.

Stories are told of how the Marquis de Lafayette was entertained at the Old Seabrook Mansion while touring the South in
1825. Before the great Frenchman stepped ashore, a carpet was
spread a distance of a quarter-mile from the boat landing to the
house, so the general would not have to put his foot on common
soil. Area planters attended a reception in his honor. Whitmarsh
Benjamin Seabrook, a distinguished speaker, made the welcom-
ing address.

It was during that reception that the daughter of Lafayette's
hosts was christened. Lafayette requested the honor of naming
William Seabrook's infant daughter, whom he called Carolina de
Lafayette Seabrook. That same child later married James
Hopkinson, a grandson of Francis Hopkinson, a signer of the

Declaration of Independence and the designer of the American flag.

The island's churches are as illustrious as its plantations.

The earliest records of Edisto Island Presbyterian Church date from 1790, but its beginnings were probably much earlier, as there was mention of a Presbyterian church on the island as early as 1710. This structure has the distinction of being the oldest Presbyterian church in its original location in South Carolina. Its charter was granted on March 26, 1784. The congregation outgrew the church during the golden age of sea-island cotton, so a new building was constructed; so generous were the planter families that the builder was given a bonus of three hundred dollars. Renovations were made in 1836, thanks to a bequest of five thousand dollars from William Seabrook. The church was refurnished in 1863.

The graveyard behind the church holds the remains of some of the island's most prosperous planters. One tombstone marks the resting place of Arthur Alfred Gilling, killed in a duel on Edingsville Beach. The remains of three New Englanders also lie here. They came to Edisto during the Civil War to teach freedmen but were killed on Christmas night 1865 in a boating accident on St. Pierre Creek.

Edisto Island Baptist Church was founded by Mrs. Hephzibah Jenkins Townsend, a woman still remembered on the island. She was a dyed-in-the-wool Baptist and her husband was a Presbyterian, so they argued frequently. Their most serious disagreement came when Hephzibah learned that her husband was planning to leave all his property to their eldest son. Most sea-island cotton planters believed in primogeniture, but Hephzibah felt all fourteen of their children should share in the property. Indeed, so strong was her conviction that she moved out of the family home and built another house for herself only. After her husband relented, she moved back in with him.

Trinity Episcopal Church was founded in 1774, although the name *Trinity* did not come into use until the 1830s. The first building was erected on land that once belonged to Abraham Wright. When the congregation outgrew the sanctuary, a new church was built. Trinity Episcopal had an endowment of thirty thousand dollars prior to the Civil War, but members and endowment dollars were considerably fewer after the conflict. Fire in a field spread to the church in 1876. The present structure was built and consecrated in 1881, only to be heavily damaged in a hurricane in 1893. Other hurricanes also took their toll. The roof blew off in 1940. Looking at the white wooden structure

Trinity Episcopal Church

with its red roof and steeple, modern visitors could hardly guess the history it has seen.

A large labor force was required to work the Edisto fields and serve the homes of the planters. The slaves brought religious rites and superstitions with them from Africa, some of which are still honored on the island. Belief was strong in five creatures that roamed the woodlands at night: "hags," "hants," "boo-daddies," "plat-eye," and ghosts.

"Oh, I have all sorta experience with hag," said Maulsey Stoney of Edisto Island. Hags were said to be real people who slipped out of their skin at midnight and went about tormenting acquaintances. They "rode" their victims and sucked blood from their necks. "First time hag ride me, I been a young gal," Stoney recalled. "Some enemy put hag up to the devilment, I know. In them day and time, young men come around for to court and gal chillun follow you. I 'spect one of them gal chillun ain't like it 'cause certain boy love me very much, and she set hag on my track. And that not all. That same hag ride me for thirty-three nights. My nerves were so worked down that I fell away to skin and bone. Scarcely got wink of sleep all night long."

A young woman remembered how her father, a favorite victim of hags, would cry out in the night. Her mother would shake the man awake, screaming, "Leave my husband alone, you hag!" One day, a woman whom the family believed to be a hag arrived for a visit. The children decided to test the theory that a hag would never cross a broom without stopping to count the straws—and that a hag never had time to count so many straws. Thus, brooms were thought to be a hag deterrent. After the woman was comfortably seated and well into a conversation, the children placed a broom across the front door. Hours later, they finally removed the broom, at which time the woman promptly left. In that manner, the family was convinced she was a hag.

A former slave who worked in the Cassina Point area of Edisto Island told an amusing ghost story to Chalmers S. Murray of Charleston in 1937:

> Oh, I was to tell you 'bout that mean trick the ghost play on me last year. It happen like this: I been 'tend meeting that night. We have nice time. Deacon August Mannery hold forth and all we give testimony. Cain't say why hard luck track me. Maybe I ain't come out plain with my testimony. Anyhow, five minutes after I leave the crossroads, a ghost butt me.
>
> It been sharp cold and I got on my brand-new overcoat my wife's cousin's child send me from New York. I know full well that overcoat going to hold me back. I start run like I crazy, but too much weight been across my shoulder. The ghost close in on me. I jump out of the road and dodge behind toothache tree [prickly ash]. The ghost follow me. I break loose again and make for Bear Hog Bottom, where them high cypress trees grow. I think I can hide somewhere in that swamp, 'cause ghosts don't like for cross water. I make big mistake. The mud awful deep and I bog down. Ghost ain't far behind me. No time for tarry. I loose my shoe and pull one foot out, then the other. I back on the road again, thank the Lawd.
>
> I look back and see a big white thing bigger than a cow. That thing could run. My tongue been hang out till it almost touch the ground. The ghost slip up and grab me from the back and I swear I lose then. But I very nimble and I slip out my overcoat right quick and jump. I leave the ghost a-holding

onto my overcoat and get away from that place. I done get my second wind and I keep going and turn in at my brother's house.

I never see my brand-new overcoat again. Swear to God, I ain't know what a ghost want with overcoat 'cause they don't wear no clothes. Anyhow, he got it and he keep it, and I ain't going to follow no ghost to hell for a overcoat, no sir.

That just show you how ghost stand. Torment the living spirit out of a man. I 'counter all kind of ghosts in my life, but that the first one I meet that got a thiefing habit.

Members of the old Edisto families played an important part in the Civil War. In fact, some claim that Edisto Island was responsible for South Carolina's withdrawal from the Union.

When there was still some hesitancy about signing the Ordinance of Secession, Colonel Joseph Jenkins of Brick House, delegate from Edisto, proclaimed, "If South Carolina refuses to secede from the Union, Edisto Island will!" According to Isaac Jenkins Mikell, that remark settled the matter for South Carolina, which voted to leave the Union and thus saved Edisto from being "the Independent Republic of Edisto Island," with fifty square miles of territory and five thousand inhabitants, forty-six hundred of them slaves. Had South Carolina and the entire South not chosen secession, Edisto residents might have found themselves with either a brand-new nation or the most one-sided war in the history of the world.

At the outbreak of hostilities, orders were dispatched for units to guard the mouths of the rivers leading to Charleston Harbor, including the North Edisto River. One day, news was received that Federal gunboats were approaching the coast near Edisto. In response, an artillery regiment proceeded toward the inlet, some of the men riding to their post in carriages.

When camp was made, a dispute arose as to which men were to take sentry duty. A tempting repast had been prepared by the body servants of the Edisto soldiers, and no one felt inclined to give up his place at the table. A compromise was finally reached. The officers decided that no sentries would be posted during meal hours. This suited the whole company, and they fell to eating. As it turned out, no enemy ships appeared that day or in the following days, and the planters returned to their homes.

Late in 1861, Confederate general Robert E. Lee deemed it impossible to defend the coastal strip from Charleston to Florida. Federal gunboats were patrolling St. Helena Sound when the Mikells of Peter's Point decided to make a mad dash for the safety of their Charleston mansion. Their boat was propelled by twelve oarsmen, who rowed to the limit of their endurance to deliver the Mikells and their children to safety.

Throughout the war, the island was occupied by United States Army regiments from Ohio, Massachusetts, and New Hampshire. Some of the elaborate furnishings in the planters' homes were stolen. When the Mikells returned after the war, they were pleased to find that their buildings had suffered less damage than those of other planters whose homes had been occupied. Cassina Point, the stately Carolina de Lafayette Hopkinson home, was one of those occupied. The gardens of the Old Seabrook Mansion were devastated by raiders from General William T. Sherman's army, who also painted graffiti on the walls.

In the closing days of the war, Sherman's Special Order 15

commandeered a zone of coastline thirty miles wide from Charleston to Florida, to be used as a refuge for former slaves. More than ten thousand ill, down-and-out former slaves—men, women, and children—came to Edisto. They were crowded into homes such as the Old Seabrook Mansion. The mansions were communal dwellings, a family occupying each room. The dining room was usually designated a "Praise House." Sometimes, the sideboard was used as a pulpit.

The freedmen were bewildered, as military authorities had failed to draw up plans sufficient to care for them. Fortunately, philanthropic societies in New England, composed mostly of abolitionists deeply concerned with the desperate situation of the former slaves, sent missionaries and teachers to Beaufort. From there, a number of them made their way to Edisto Island.

Expecting to find large plantations and beautiful homes, they were in for a surprise. The fields had not been cultivated for four years, and equipment was lying in decay. Authorities had given the freedmen all the land that had belonged to the planters.

The missionaries opened a commissary in a vacant building and distributed rations to the freedmen. Nicholas Blaisdell, a teacher, took over California Plantation on St. Pierre Creek and used it as a school. Another man who came to help in the relief work was James Pierpont Blake of Connecticut, a grandson of Eli Whitney, inventor of the cotton gin. Blake had contracted polio while at Yale and was crippled by the disease. Another missionary was Emily Bliss, who took over James Whaley Plantation and opened a school on the front porch. Adults as well as children attended the Edisto Island schools. One day, a man was observed reading from a book he held upside down. He said that was all right, as he intended to learn to read "every which ways."

Finally, information came to the authorities that the former owners were to repossess their plantations. All freedmen on the island were called to a meeting and told that President Andrew Johnson had no power to prevent the planters from reclaiming their land, as the island had been taken over by General Sherman by a war order and not by an act of Congress. Disbelief spread among the freedmen as they were told they could sign contracts and be paid wages to work the land for the planters.

Ordered to vacate the houses, the freedmen camped out by the hundreds, awaiting transportation from the island. The last building to be surrendered was Edisto Island Presbyterian Church. The Reverend William States Lee found that his church had been abused, its pipe organ stolen. Some sacred books taken from the church were later returned.

The planters gradually came back and took over their estates, and some freedmen returned to work for their former masters. But the days when sea-island cotton was king were past. When the boll weevil made its appearance in 1919, cotton production passed into history. Edisto Islanders then gave their attention to cattle raising and the production of nuts, fruits, and other crops.

Some islanders learned to subsist off the waters. Catching fish became an important part of the lives of slave descendants. In fact, they made a ritual of fishing and could tell you exactly what you should do to have the best luck.

Some days were luckier than others. There were certain things you should say when you threw your line out and when you brought it in. There were people you should talk to before going fishing and others you should avoid. For instance, a fisherman should never talk with an old woman before casting, and by no means should any old person handle the line the day before it was used. On the other hand, it was lucky to talk with a young girl before you started.

If you left something behind and started back after it, you would catch few fish that day. Thus, you should abandon your fishing if you forgot your line or net or box of hooks.

You should never bring a dog fishing with you. Fish did not like dogs—or cats either, for that matter.

You should never grumble about your luck. If you finally caught a measly catfish the length of your finger after fishing for several hours, you shouldn't swear. Instead, you should say in a loud voice, "Thank God for that."

You shouldn't carry food with you or eat while you fished, for the fish would believe you were not badly in need of sustenance and would not come to your line.

It was best not to have a woman with you on a fishing trip.

The descendants of Edisto slaves knew these rules and would never think of violating them. But a few people possessed fishing secrets they were loath to reveal. "Ain't for to tell all you know, 'cause iffen you do, everybody will be just as lucky as you," a man on Seabrook Plantation said. "A man who make he living off fishin' got to be careful."

Robert Samuel maintained he was the best fisherman at Seaside Plantation because he possessed stones that enabled him to catch any fish that swam in the waters. "See this here bag?" he once said, referring to the tobacco sack he carried with him. "I got stone from every fish that live in the creek. As long as I carry this bag with me, I draw fish to me. That's how I so lucky." Inside the bag was a collection of small, oval-shaped, well-polished stones of varying size. Samuel claimed to have collected them from his previous victims: "Every kind of fish I catch, I split him, laid him open, and took the stone out."

An "eagle stone" was said to be even more powerful than a fish stone. Whereas the latter only attracted fish, an eagle stone would draw almost any object you could name. Eagle stones were rare, and the people who owned them were regarded with respect and awe. Procuring an eagle stone was attended with danger. Some people claimed the stones were to be found at the bottom of an eagle's nest, while others said they had to be cut from an eagle's throat. George Brown of Edisto Island took the latter view, as revealed in the story he once told of his friend Charles Green's dangerous climb up a tree in search of a stone:

> When Charles get to the tiptop branch of the tree, he find the nest. The eagle ain't been home then. So Charles search the nest careful, but he ain't find nothing. Just as he fix to climb down, please God, the eagle show up! That been the devil's den, sure enough. The bird flew round and round Charles and beat him with a wing. Then he start to peck him, but that man got plenty of nerve. He manage to draw a knife and cut the bird in the throat. Then what you think happen? Charles see the stone pop out the eagle throat and fall plop on the ground. The eagle flew away screeching 'cause he done lose he power, and Charles come on down the tree. He pick up the stone off the ground and run with it. If you ain't believe me, ask Charles. He got the stone in his trunk now, wrapped in a leaf from the Bible.

In the mid-1930s, the fish took a three-year vacation. Anglers counted themselves lucky if they could bring in a few small croakers and a tiny whiting as the result of a full day's labor. Crabs appeared in small numbers, and shrimp were at a premium. A large proportion of the populace depended upon seafood, and poor families on Edisto were going hungry.

Most local fishermen believed it was the presence of shrimp trawlers that was responsible for the decrease in the number of fish. Complaints were made to the board of fisheries, and Edisto fishermen were assured that everything possible would be done to apprehend offenders. A law went into effect that trawlers had to stay three miles offshore. According to Edisto anglers, that kept the commercial shrimpers from destroying thousands of fish destined for the island's inlets.

By 1937, the fish were back. Shrimp were running and plump croakers were biting. Amateur anglers could generally catch enough croakers for a meal in thirty minutes of fishing. Spotted trout, which usually didn't start running until the middle of August, were reported as early as the first week in July. Anglers brought in fish as long as the bait held out.

The following year, millions of transparent fish less than an inch in length were released into the broad waters of the Edisto River from the shad hatchery at Jacksonboro, operated jointly by the state and federal bureaus of fisheries. To restock the river, shad had been caught by fishermen employed by the state bureau, which furnished the eggs. The federal government, which maintained the hatchery, had then hatched the roe.

In 1939, some Edisto anglers committed the heresy of fishing for sea trout with artificial bait. As far back as the memories of islanders ran, no angler had tried to take a fish in the salt streams near the ocean with anything but porgies, clams, mullet, or shrimp. During that season, however, uplanders anxious to secure their quota of winter trout introduced the islanders to a new trick.

At first, the people of Edisto would have nothing to do with the gaily painted clothespin lures. No self-respecting fish would strike at a piece of wood, they said. But before December came to an end, a few islanders bought rods, reels, and wooden lures and began practicing. Success attended their efforts. More trout were caught that month than the fishermen had seen in several years combined. George Seabrook, Jr., reported that he caught eighty-six in about as many minutes. Within weeks, almost everyone on the island was talking about buying the newfangled outfits.

The 1930s also saw the solution of a longtime problem on Edisto Island.

Before the Civil War, a causeway was thrown up in the Dawhoo marshlands to afford passage between Edisto and the mainland for carriages, carts, and wagons. Even in the days when heavy vehicles were unknown, the surface—a few feet of shells and dirt over unexplored depths of decayed vegetable matter—refused to stay put. Many a carriage or wagon bogged axle-deep in the mud and had to be hauled out by manpower. Shortly before the war, the causeway was abandoned.

In 1914, the causeway through the marshes was rebuilt. It was a mud road, much to the discomfort of everyone who crossed it. Motorists were often forced to gather loose timber from the marshes and build a sort of wooden road before they could proceed. On one occasion, a party of young men from Charleston tried to cross the causeway on a hot, sticky summer night. Discovering that they would have to shove their car for about a mile through the mud, they removed everything but their underclothes. Mosquitoes set their skin on fire, but they would not dress, fearing injury to their suits. Upon reaching firmer ground, they rode the rest of the way to the southern end of the island in their scanty attire. The automobile was shipped back by boat the next day.

"I know that brackish water marsh well," remarked an old Edisto resident when the causeway was being rebuilt yet again. "There simply is no bottom. I've seen a mule suddenly slip down through that mud until only his ears were showing." Another Edisto Islander said he had seen a man sink a thirty-foot pole through the causeway and still not reach the bottom.

Matters came to a head when the elements started misbehaving. For time untold, Edisto had generally experienced droughts in the spring, but the 1930s were the grand exception. For days, it would rain—hard, pelting rain that reduced even solid roads to quagmires. The Dawhoo causeway didn't stand a chance.

The causeway was a universal subject of conversation among the island folk. Enough suggestions were made about the proper way to rebuild it to fill half a dozen volumes. When engineers arrived at a permanent solution around 1937, the islanders finally had a hard, smooth, all-weather surface. The keen satisfaction they experienced could not possibly be appreciated by an outsider. And the main road down the island—for many years a curving, rutted affair where vision was difficult due to the many overhanging live oaks—was straightened and modernized. In the view of many, the improved roads brought Edisto Island fully into the modern world.

Its great plantations have always been what defined Edisto. Today, visitors will find them in varying states of repair. Peter's Point, the home of the Mikell family, remains, though not in its original form. Brick House, credited with being the first manor house built in America, burned in 1929, but the vine-covered walls that remain standing are impressive enough to justify a short ride on Brick House Road to view them. The property is still owned by the Jenkins family. The Old Seabrook Mansion was owned in later years by Donald D. Dodge of Philadelphia, whose descendants use it today. It is the only island mansion that has been completely restored to its original grandeur. Cassina Point is also well preserved.

Some of the old manor houses are just memories. Sea Cloud and Bleak Hall are now used as a hunting preserve. Sea Cloud House—named for the families of the couple who built it, the Seabrooks and the McLeods—was abandoned and then dismantled. Bleak Hall—so named because of its owner's fondness for the Charles Dickens novel *Bleak House*—was torn down. Some of the barns, stables, and storage houses of Bleak Hall were saved and are now listed on the National Register of Historic Places.

The best time to view the old mansions and ruins is the second Saturday in October, when the annual Island Tour of Historic Plantations and Churches is held.

LADY'S ISLAND

Lady's Island bridge

As with most of South Carolina's sea islands, the story of Lady's Island, off Beaufort, is one of plantations made prosperous by the labor of slaves. Here is how Sam Mitchell, a slave on Woodlawn Plantation, owned by John Chaplin, described slave life on the island:

> Mr. Chaplin had seven plantations. He lived at Brickyard Plantation in winter and in Beaufort in summer. He had many slaves. As near as I can remember, he had fifteen slaves on Woodlawn Plantation.

Slave cabins had two rooms. In our house was bed, table, and bench to sit on. My father made them. My mother had fourteen children. Us sleep on floor.

Every Tuesday, Master give each slave a peck of corn. When potato dug, we got potato. Two times in the year, we got six yards of cloth, calico in spring and homespun in the winter. Once a year, we got shoes. A slave had land to cultivate for himself, and we could raise a pig.

My father had a boat, and he went fishing at night and sold the fish. Master let him cut post and wood at night and sell that. In the daytime, he had to do his task. He was carpenter, but he also plowed the fields. My mother hoed.

On Woodlawn, there was no overseer. Master didn't allow much whipping, but slave had to do task. If didn't, then he get whipping. Driver do whipping, but if he whip too severely, Master would sometime take field hand and make him driver and put driver in the field.

If a slave was sick, Master would come and see what was the matter. If he was sick, Master would take him to Beaufort to the doctor. If a woman slave was sick, Big Missus would go and see her.

Slaves had only one holiday in the year. That was Christmas. Master would kill a cow on every plantation on Christmas and give all slaves some.

On Master John Chaplin's plantations, a slave had to tell him as soon as he began to court. If Master say, "No, you can't marry that gal," then that settled it. He didn't like for his slaves to marry slaves on another person's plantation, and if you did that, you had to get a pass from Master to visit your wife. When slaves married, a white preacher married them in Master Chaplin's house.

Slaves had their own church on the plantation, but on Communion Sunday, you had to go to white folks' church in Beaufort and sit upstairs.

Master had nine children. Six boys were in Rebel army. That Wednesday in November when gun was first shot at Bay Point, I thought it was thunder rolling, but there was no cloud. My mother say, "Son, that ain't no thunder. Yankee come to give you freedom." I been so glad I jump up and down and ran around.

After freedom, everybody did as he pleased. The Yankee opened school for former slaves, and the teacher lived in Master's house at Brickyard Plantation. My father got job as carpenter with Yankee and bought ten acres of land on Lady's Island.

The tradition of Lady's Island oystering goes back to the Indians, who left evidence of their oyster roasts. An oyster factory was established on the island in 1891 by Captain Thomas L. Swinton. Swinton sold the factory to R. K. Harley, who ran it for many years. Oysters were gathered from boats with a "grab," or hook, and sold to factories by the bushel, two hundred bushels usually being bought at one time. At the factories, women bandaged their hands against sharp shells and removed the oysters after steaming. Carefully sorted, the oysters were washed and put into cans of brine, sealed, labeled, and shipped to Northern markets. Oyster shells were also used in roadbeds and were ground for chicken feed and fertilizer.

The completion of a bridge in 1927 established an overland connection between Lady's Island and the mainland.

Colony Gardens, a two-and-a-half-story clubhouse, was erected at Cuthbert Point in 1931 to attract Northern visitors. It faced a broad stretch of river, and the town of Beaufort was visible in the distance. A double-deck piazza flanked three sides of the clubhouse. At the rear was a saltwater swimming pool. An added attraction was the old plantation house nearby, a one-story frame structure on a high basement. It had a hip roof, flared entrance steps, and square columns on its brick-pillared piazza.

Terror seized Lady's Island in 1936 when it was learned that the body of a child who was a victim of meningitis was being sent to the island from Charleston County for burial. Beaufort County health officials and police officers stationed themselves at the outskirts of Beaufort at dawn. When the funeral party finally arrived, it was escorted through the city under guard so that none of the members could come into contact with others.

After the party made its way across the bridge onto Lady's Island, a minister was found plowing his field. He was barely allowed time to dash into his house, inform his wife, put on a coat to cover his overalls, and grab his Sunday hat. Then the party proceeded to the cemetery. Members of the child's family gathered at the burial site. The law-enforcement officers guarding the remains made it hard for the mourners to convey their sympathy.

When the time came to lower the little coffin into the grave, there were no volunteers among the men in the funeral party. No one would touch the coffin. Finally, a policeman took one end and commanded the bereaved father to take the other.

Then came the nerve-racking return to Charleston. There, too, the sad group was met at the bridge and ushered into the city under guard.

A happier event occurred on Lady's Island that same year when Bobby Mayo, seven-year-old son of Mr. and Mrs. Oscar Mayo, caught a large sea bat—a specimen rarely, if ever, seen on the island—with an ordinary hook and line. It took father, mother, and son to pull the bat in. Even then, it would have been lost if not for a blow from a stick. The wounded bat struggled back to the water but plunged blindly into the bank and was captured. The strange creature weighed nearly fifty pounds and was one of about fifteen found floundering in shallow water near the Mayo home. Snapshots were made of the sea monster and its young captor.

Today, Lady's Island is known for its scenic vistas and its many excellent restaurants and shopping opportunities.

ST. HELENA ISLAND

The Indians called the water wonderland around Beaufort the "Country of a Hundred Islands." There are at least sixty-five islands here, and they have played important roles not only in the history of the area but in the history of all South Carolina. The islands include Horse Island, where a mixed breed of English and Chickasaw horses was developed; Bermuda, named for the English island from which some of its planters migrated; Hog Island, where swine were raised; Chisolm Island, known as Pacific Island when it was the property of the Pacific Guano Company; Buzzard's Island, named for the birds that used it for their nesting place; Dataw (pronounced Daw-taw) Island, an exclusive private community that was once the site of the first commercial orange grove in America; Morgan Island; Lemon Island; Spring Island; Polwanna Island; and others.

Some of the islands are privately owned. Others have upscale housing areas. Many have been washed away. An example of the latter is Egg Island—also called Eggbank Island—located off St. Helena Island's Coffin Point Plantation. Egg Island was so small that it could be circled by boat in less than half an hour. It was once a government-owned sanctuary where thousands of birds came to lay their eggs and hatch their young. Walking on it was impossible during nesting season, as it was completely covered in eggs. The beach along the water's edge was strewn with the skeletons of great sea turtles, and the air was alive with the chatter of birds, from sandpipers to pelicans. At some point, the island, which had always seemed too frail to hold back the mighty ocean, was completely washed away. No trace of it is left.

St. Helena is one of South Carolina's largest sea islands. Its history goes back to the time before European exploration. Indian Hill on St. Helena is said to be a burial mound. An Indian chief's funeral was supposedly held here. His body was strapped to his favorite horse, and the members of the tribe threw handfuls of sand on the figures until they were entombed and a hill raised.

The mound stood in the center of cultivated fields and was a landmark known near and far. It was thirteen feet high, and the summit plateau was sixty-two feet across and perfectly level. From the northern side, a trench eighteen feet wide ran along the base to the center of the mound, composed of a mixture of sand and clay.

The first South Carolina island seen by non-Indians may have been St. Helena Island, as it is called today, or Punta de Santa

Elena, as it was called by Francisco Gordillo. Some people believe that this young Spanish captain, attached to the explorer Lucas Vasquez de Ayllon, reached the island in 1520 and named it for the day it was discovered—Santa Elena's Day, August 18. Others believe it was first seen by Spanish sailors under Angel de Villafane on Santa Elena's Day in 1561.

William Hilton and the English immigrants who followed him found St. Helena excellent for the production of indigo, rice, and sea-island cotton. St. Helena cotton was so exceptional that some planters shipped their harvest directly to the best English spinners. The cotton culture created a powerful and restricted caste of plantation nobles who built fine manor houses. The island planters spent much of their time in Beaufort, leaving crop production in the hands of overseers.

Ebenezer Coffin, a New Englander, settled Coffin Point Plantation during the 1790s, when sea-island cotton was just getting a toehold as a crop. Coffin's fine home was raised well off the ground and had a six-columned piazza overlooking St. Helena Sound. By 1813, some 232 acres were planted in cotton at Coffin Point.

Frogmore Plantation was granted to William Bull in 1731. It had seventy-eight slaves in 1800, giving it the largest slave community on St. Helena. In 1815, 133 bales of sea-island cotton left Frogmore Plantation for the Charleston market. William J. Grayson bought Frogmore in 1836, at which time it was valued at thirty thousand dollars. Grayson is believed to have been the largest producer of cotton in the area, followed by the Coffins of Coffin Point and the Chaplins of Tombee.

John Fripp started out on Fripp Island in the late 1600s. He and his wife, Sarah, came to be the largest landowners on St. Helena. They began planting around 1725. One of the largest families on the island, the Fripps owned more than twelve thousand acres on St. Helena and the surrounding islands by 1860. Tidalholm, an elegant townhouse in Beaufort, was the property of Edgar Fripp.

Another St. Helena family, the Chaplins, also began planting around 1725. Their plantation, Tombee, was named to honor Tom B. Chaplin, the man who built the family home around 1795. The manor house at Tombee is still in existence.

St. Helena Island experienced a taste of international excitement in 1815, when Napoleon was forced to live on the island of the same name located off West Africa. When the planters on South Carolina's St. Helena heard about the famous man's exile, they assumed he was headed for their island and flatly told the world they would have no part of Napoleon's contaminating influence. Slaves on St. Helena and Edisto also heard the rumors. Finally, an old slave on Edisto Island offered a solution. "Iffen the people on St. Helena's Island won't have Poleon on their island, very well," he said. "Just put him on Edisto, and first thing you know, him done set we free."

Most members of the close-knit planter society attended St. Helena Episcopal Church. The members of that church also erected the tabby structure known as the Old White Church, which served as a "chapel of ease" for plantation owners in St. Helena Parish who lived too far from Beaufort to attend church there. Though the Old White Church burned in 1865, enough of it is left to give visitors an idea of what it once looked like. The graveyard and its mausoleums also remain.

Old White Church

In 1855, planters of the Baptist persuasion built Brick Baptist Church on what was then John Fripp's Corner Plantation. The church had a gallery for favored slaves. The slave population preferred the Baptist faith. At that time, there were 3,557 black Baptists in the Beaufort area and only 156 white Baptists. Brick Baptist Church was abandoned by the planters in 1861, at which time blacks moved their services there. More often than not, they were led by a white minister.

In 1850, St. Helena Parish produced more than a million pounds of cotton. The princely life enjoyed by the planters was built upon slave labor, their elaborate houses constructed in the certainty that there would always be plenty of slaves to care for them. But with emancipation and the passage of the island into Union hands

Brick Baptist Church

early in the Civil War, life on St. Helena changed forever.

When Union forces seized nearby Hilton Head Island and began using it as a base of operations for their blockading fleet, the St. Helena planters fled inland, at which time their property was confiscated by the Federal government. Soon afterward, a group of abolitionists inaugurated the Port Royal Experiment to provide the ten thousand blacks who remained in the area with opportunities for education and self-sufficiency. Cotton-growing operations on the plantations continued. Now, however, the former slaves were paid for their labor.

In 1862, Laura Towne and Ellen Murray, missionaries from the North, came to St. Helena and established the Penn School, the first local school for blacks, housed in a ready-made building sent all the way from Philadelphia. Penn was an industrial school where boys and girls were taught to be farmers and homemakers, to build and sew, to weave baskets of sweet grass and cook. Many of the Penn School teachers were trained on the premises. Other graduates were sent to the various county schools on St. Helena and other islands to teach. A nurse and a farm and home agent worked through the school to teach sanitation and better methods of farming to the islanders.

Each fall, a fair was held at the school. The Penn School also presented a community "sing" on the third Sunday of each month, giving islanders an opportunity to gather and sing old-time spirituals and visitors an opportunity to hear spirituals as only the islanders could sing them.

In the late 1940s, a public high school opened on St. Helena, and the private Penn School saw falling enrollment. It graduated its last class in 1953. The school began a new life when it reopened as the Penn Center, whose purpose was to provide services related to health care, land preservation, and community enrichment. The Penn Center also saw use as a retreat. The late Dr. Martin Luther King, Jr., met here with other black leaders to plan the 1963 march on Washington and the 1965 march on Selma. Former president Jimmy Carter has also used the facility.

The Penn School was only one of many changes brought to St. Helena by the Civil War. On March 9, 1863, tax commissioners held a land sale on St. Helena. Thousands of acres of plantation lands were confiscated and sold. Eleven plantations were bought by one man, Edward Philbrick. Other parcels were set aside by the government for military properties and school farms. The rest was surveyed into small plots and sold to the heads of black families. By June 1865, there were 347 purchases on St. Helena, 243 of them in 10-acre tracts. Eliza H. Chaplin, a member of one of the old planter families, redeemed 5 acres

Penn Center

of a plantation which had originally contained 400 acres. Edgar Fripp redeemed 732 acres of an estate which had comprised 1,284 acres.

The plight of the planters is best captured in the story of Edgar Fripp and Tidalholm, his lovely, spacious home in Beaufort. After the war, when many families were at a loss to regain their property, a wealthy Frenchman was in the garden of Tidalholm when it was being auctioned for taxes. As he watched, a disheveled man tottered into the yard. When the Frenchman asked who he was, he replied that he was Edgar Fripp and that he had returned to see his house sold, as he had no funds with which to make a bid. The Frenchman quickly bid on and won the home. When he was given the title, he took it to Edgar Fripp and pressed it into his hand. "I didn't fight for the cause, but now I feel I've done my duty to help the American South," he said. He then left Beaufort, giving no name or address.

In the years following the war, a good part of the land on

St. Helena—both that remaining in the planter families and that acquired by former slaves—was sold to Northern sportsmen for use as hunting preserves. Still, hundreds of small landowners held onto their estates.

In 1898, during the Spanish-American War, Fort Fremont was constructed on St. Helena. For a short time, it bustled with men in uniform and the sounds of fife and drum, but as the threat of war diminished, its concrete bastions and gun emplacements were abandoned. Bats rustled through unused subterranean passages, and snakes slithered into the sunlight. In fact, Fort Fremont was so hidden by wild shrubbery that it appeared to be nothing but a great mound of earth and bushes. The property then passed into the hands of Fred J. Barnes. Under his ownership, the under-growth was kept down, and the walls of the picturesque old fort could be clearly seen by people approaching on Land's End Road. Some visitors felt they were coming upon a scene from medieval times.

For many years, one could view the wiry little horses of St. Helena, believed by some to have deteriorated from fine plantation stock and by others to have been introduced by the Spanish. They ran wild over the island, living mainly on marsh grass. Before the automobile, these "tackies" pulled carts over the unpaved roadways.

The island neighborhood of Frogmore has been called "the Witchcraft Capital of the World," perhaps because the famous (and infamous) Dr. Buzzard lived and practiced his irregular medicine there. One of the many colorful stories about Dr. Buzzard tells of how, during World War II, he was brought to trial for allegedly preparing and distributing a potion that would make young men's heart rate and blood pressure soar. Taken shortly before their medical examination for military service, the brew kept them from being inducted. Those were patriotic times, and public sentiment was heavily against Dr. Buzzard when he took the stand in court and admitted his guilt. The judge sentenced him to five years in prison or a five-thousand-dollar fine. The war years were lean times, so everyone in attendance was astonished when Dr. Buzzard removed a roll of bills from the inside pocket of his coat, counted off fifty hundred-dollar notes, and asked the judge if a cash payment was acceptable.

Dr. Buzzard is gone, but some cabins on the island still have their door and window frames painted blue in order to ward off spirits.

Frogmore is also famous for its Frogmore Stew, made with potatoes, corn on the cob, onions, and shrimp.

In recent years, the St. Helena fields that once grew sea-island cotton have become the center of a rich farming area. The local tomato crop is one of the largest in the county.

The manor house at Coffin Point Plantation stands regally today, facing the sea. The three-story white clapboard mansion with the red roof commands a sweeping view of the ocean, the sky, and Edisto Island in the distance. On clear nights, its lights can be seen many miles at sea.

The house was once used as an officers' club by the military brass at nearby Parris Island. United States senator J. M. Cameron of Pennsylvania later bought it after viewing its hand-carved moldings and graceful curving stairway.

During the 1950s, J. E. McTeer bought Coffin Point. The sheriff of Beaufort County since before he turned twenty, McTeer was by then in his eighth term. He was also a noted collector of guns, swords, and other relics—enough to fill an entire room at Coffin Point. His collection of guns traced an almost unbroken history of American firearms from the blunderbuss of the sixteenth century to weapons of the late 1930s. Among Sheriff McTeer's collection of Colt pistols—said to be the finest known—were the largest Colt ever made and a silver-engraved model once presented to King George of England. The Colt of which he was most proud once belonged to Confederate general Wade Hampton. The inscription on it read, "Captured by Lt. Genl. Hampton, presented to Genl. J. E. Johnston. Exchanged by him to John L. Fairly, Ad. C., at request of former, April 18, 1865." Among McTeer's other collections were a Crusader's sword, a mastodon kneecap, a rib from a woolly mammoth, and a tooth weighing five pounds.

Sheriff McTeer was only one of the many interesting people to own a St. Helena plantation during the twentieth century.

With its old houses, old churches, old families, and traces of good times and bad, today's St. Helena could qualify as a museum, each of its side roads revealing unexpected landmarks.

Tropical vegetation abounds on Hunting Island.

HUNTING ISLAND

Hunting Island is part of the chain of Capers, Fripp, Pritchard, St. Phillip, and Bay Point Islands. These islands were once collectively called "the Hunting Islands," in view of their abundant wildlife and the hunting parties held on them.

The islands' agricultural value was negligible during the colonial era, due to their low elevation and sandy soil. Instead, both locals and wealthy Northerners began acquiring them for hunting deer, ducks, turkeys, and other wildlife.

The hunting parties on four-mile-long Hunting Island are the stuff of legend. They usually lasted several days. Wives were welcome if they cared to enjoy the hunters' paradise. The daytime was reserved for expeditions and the night for lively parties. It was said that five hundred deer roamed over the island's five thousand acres of jungle and marsh. Alligators sunned themselves beside the inlets, where pipestem-legged shorebirds stepped gingerly, stalking minnows.

The hurricane of Friday, October 13, 1893, was a major event in the history of Hunting Island. The steamship *Savannah* had an unfortunate encounter with a nearby reef. The high seas, screaming winds, and accompanying tornadoes claimed the lives of over a thousand people on the islands of Beaufort County.

The matriarch of Hunting Island is North Beach Lighthouse, built in 1873. The light flashed a 120,000-candlepower beam to ships at sea before it was retired from service. Twice in its lifetime, it has been moved away from the grasp of the ocean just as it was ready to be dragged to a watery grave. The lighthouse remains open for climbing for those bold enough to try to reach the top.

Hunting Island is now a state park with a white-sand beach and thick stands of tropical foliage. Actually, the park nearly passed from existence in the early 1960s, when the effects of countless storms coupled with a lack of upkeep left it with the loss of a mile of beach and jungle, washed-away roads, a water supply declared unfit for human consumption, rental cabins not worthy of housing livestock, and broken-down maintenance equipment. Under the direction of new park supervisor Lee Jordon and Misener Marine, however, an 840-foot reinforced-concrete groin was constructed to aid the buildup of sand, dredging operations were commenced, water and sewage facilities were upgraded, cottages were renovated, pavilions were built, camping facilities were expanded, and a new lake on the island filled with fish and became a popular stop for birds.

Since that time, Hunting Island State Park has attracted more than a quarter-million people annually. Visitors witness the natural wildness that brought the place its early fame. Those who drive the roadway encircling the island are likely to see deer standing by the side of the road. And those who camp at the park find the exotic vegetation so thick that they wouldn't be surprised to see Tarzan swing by on a vine.

North Beach Lighthouse on Hunting Island

FRIPP ISLAND

Fripp Island

Fripp Island was named for the same John Fripp who planted some of the fields of St. Helena Island. Fripp was a British privateer who used his namesake island as a base of operations in the late 1600s. In fact, he was so successful that King George gave him the island.

Many of Fripp's descendants still live in South Carolina. Some are buried in nearby island churchyards. No one knows just where John Fripp is buried, but it is said that his ghost occasionally returns to Fripp Island. Unexplained boot prints have been seen on the sandy beach, leading romantic beachcombers to believe that Fripp has come back for his buried treasure. In fact, one man puts so much faith in the tale that he refuses to stay in his luxury home alone.

The island's dunes, inlets, and bluffs made it a perfect place for Edward Teach—better known as Blackbeard, the infamous pirate—to bury chests of treasure. Blackbeard preyed on the rich South Carolina trade and retreated to the inlets and lagoons, where he could not be found. Some tourists still look for his treasure chests in the wilderness.

A favorite Fripp Island story concerns Blackbeard. One day, the pirate was walking the streets of Charles Town when he spied a young woman he immediately desired as his wife. Never one to stand on ceremony, he snatched her up and carried her to his ship, though she fought fiercely every step of the way. They sailed to North Carolina, where Governor Charles Eden, a friend of Blackbeard's, married them over the young woman's energetic protests. From there, they sailed to Fripp Island, where Blackbeard left his brokenhearted bride under guard while he went back to sea. He returned to Fripp frequently and lavished precious gems on her. Finally, she became more at ease with him and reconciled herself to his line of work. In fact, they are said to have enjoyed oyster roasts on the beach. One day, she requested she be taken to the West Indies, and Blackbeard complied. It is presumed that she lived happily ever after—or at least until Blackbeard's violent death in 1718.

Another famous man figures in the legends of Fripp Island. For more than two hundred years, there has been speculation about the final resting place of Revolutionary War brigadier general Casimir Pulaski, a Polish patriot who served on the American side. In the middle of the twentieth century, interest focused on a grave discovered on a high bluff on Fripp Island. Preliminary reports seemed to suggest that it contained Pulaski's corpse. However, the findings were ultimately inconclusive, and the mystery continues.

During the Civil War, Fripp Island was confiscated by the Union for "nonpayment of the Direct tax." Julia M. Prioleau restored the island's good name by paying $4.00 in back taxes, a $2.00 penalty, $.30 in miscellaneous costs, and $.37 in interest, making the total price of redeeming the island $6.67, an unspeakable bargain in view of today's property values on Fripp.

Recalling his first glimpse of Fripp Island, new owner Jack L. Kilgore remarked, "When I saw that beach, I like to flipped." When Kilgore took over in 1960, his first task was to carve a path through the jungle covering the island. "We floated a bulldozer over on a barge and used an aerial photograph and a compass to start clearing," he recounted.

Kilgore called on a Savannah financier for help in planning a bridge to the island. The man's response was less than enthusiastic. The next time Kilgore called, he was able to say he had already raised a portion of the money, and the financier then added his contribution to the pot. A privately owned $500,000 bridge linking Fripp and Hunting Islands with the mainland was officially opened in the spring of 1964.

But before development began, there was one problem to address: wild boars. For many generations, Hampshire, Duroc-Jersey, and Poland China hogs had been running free on the island. These animals were huge, truculent, wily, and vicious. Fearing the boars with their gleaming tusks might attack humans, as they had done on mainland plantations, the owners killed about two hundred of them. The largest of all and the last to be disposed of was an especially ferocious boar called Big John. He was finally tracked to his den on the edge of a marsh.

With the boars gone, the island proved itself attractive to home buyers. The Gulf Stream, lying less than forty miles offshore, affords Fripp an average temperature of sixty-five degrees and a ten-month growing season. Like Hunting Island, three-thousand-acre Fripp Island has dense tropical vegetation that reminds some people of Hawaii. Some of the island's palmetto trees are forty-five feet high. One visitor remarked, "I haven't seen a monkey, but they've got to be around here somewhere."

People from across the United States and several foreign countries have built upscale houses on the ocean and on the site of an old cotton plantation. Noted author Pat Conroy spends much of his time here.

Probably the most popular center of activity is the island's championship golf course. Fripp Inlet and the Atlantic Ocean form scenic borders for the course, and lagoons flank the fairways. In fact, there's so much water to contend with that a retired navy captain—one of the first to swing a golf club on Fripp Island—jokingly remarked that it was a grand golf course, but that he regretted it hadn't been built on land.

Spanish explorers visited Parris Island as early as 1514.

French Huguenots led by Jean Ribaut attempted a settlement on the island in 1562.

In fact, Parris and its neighboring islands were long a bone of contention between the Spaniards and the French, perhaps because, as Ribaut put it, "there is no fayrer . . . place." So impressed was he with Port Royal Sound that he claimed it could accommodate "all of the shippes of the world."

Ribaut established a colony on Parris Island and called it Charlesfort. It has been written that, upon his arrival, he took from the Indians $1,600,000 in Spanish gold salvaged from wrecked treasure ships. That may or may not be true, but all the gold in the world wouldn't have helped him when his supplies began to dwindle sometime later. He set sail for France to replenish his provisions, leaving thirty colonists behind. Unfortunately, Ribaut found his homeland in chaos, and his return to Charlesfort was delayed.

Meanwhile, on the island, the colonists suffered from Indian attacks and illness. Many died. In an effort to prolong their lives, the survivors constructed the first ocean-worthy ship built in North America and sailed for Europe, only to have the wind die and leave them marooned in the middle of the sea. One young man, Guillaume Rouffi, elected to remain on the island with the friendly Indians. When the Spaniards landed again on Parris Island, they made Rouffi their prisoner and destroyed Charlesfort.

In 1566, the Spaniards built Fort San Felipe, which lasted ten years until it was destroyed by Indians. In 1577, they built Fort San Marcos of cedar palisades. They also captured a group of Frenchmen who landed on the island and put them to death. At that point, the Spanish settlement contained sixty houses, half of them built of tabby. Its garrison was withdrawn in 1587 due to English aggression and renewed hostilities with the Indians.

In the middle of the following century, it took twenty years of bloodshed to establish English control of this portion of the coast.

Researchers found an interesting volume in the Treasure Room—a depository for rare material at the College of Charleston—that shed light on Parris Island's early colonial days. Prepared by Jacque LeMoyne under the editorship of Theodore DeBry, the book, penned in medieval Latin, was published in 1591. LeMoyne, a Frenchman, came to the New World in 1564, when Jean Ribaut was attempting to settle Port Royal. He prepared the illustrations from rough drawings he made on what is now known as Parris Island. The book contains fine engravings that show the Indians' ideas of home and boat construction and their methods of hunting and farming.

It was from a print in this book that a monument was designed by Albert Simons and erected by the American government on what was believed to be the site of Charlesfort. The monument was unveiled in 1926 as part of a Huguenot celebration on Parris Island. However, one group has contended that the fort, excavated by United States Marines in 1917, could not possibly be the French fort, and that it is instead one erected by the Spaniards at a later date. It seems doubtful that the matter will ever be settled. But Ribaut's landing on the island in 1562 is not in dispute, and the marble shaft properly commemorates that event.

Parris Island takes its name from Alexander Parris, the public treasurer of the province of South Carolina for many years. It encompasses an area four and a half miles by six miles.

Occupying a large part of the island—and contributing heavily to the income of the county—is the Parris Island Marine Base. It is not overstating the case to say that the name *Parris Island* is synonymous with the United States Marine Corps.

The island's ties to the military go back well over a century. Parris Island was designated a United States naval station in 1876. A dry dock on the island saw its last active duty in docking the battleship *Indiana* around 1900. After 1906, the island was used as a naval prison for minor offenders. The prison was closed in the 1930s.

Initially, the government owned only about two hundred acres

Monument on supposed site of Charlesfort

of the island. That changed in 1915, when it purchased Parris Island for the sum of $248,328.68 for use as a Marine Corps training station. A fleet of small boats plied back and forth daily from St. Helena Island to Parris Island, bearing descendants of cotton-plantation slaves who were to work as laborers at the base. It was an impressive early-morning sight to witness the eight or ten boats, sails furled, headed across the river, the occupants singing spirituals in tempo with the pulling of the oars.

A year after its opening, the station was expanded for the purpose of training World War I recruits. Temporary buildings were erected to accommodate about twenty thousand men. About sixty thousand men were trained here during World War I.

That was only the beginning. Parris Island proved an ideal place for indoctrinating recruits. The mild climate and relative isolation permitted training every day of the year. Today, the base turns out nearly twenty thousand trained recruits per year. It boasts such facilities as a large hospital, a modern theater, amusement halls, restaurants, a barber shop, a library, a grammar school for children of servicemen, a chapel, clubs for officers and noncommissioned men, training schools for cooks and barbers, tennis courts, and a golf course.

Ask any "graduate," however, and he or she will assure you that Parris Island is no country club. The famous statue commemorating the five marines who raised the American flag on Iwo Jima's Mount Surabachi is on the grounds, and seeing it will give you some idea of the seriousness with which Marine Corps training is taken here. The statue's artist was Felix de Weldon, the same man who created the Iwo Jima Monument in Arlington National Cemetery. A visit to the base's museum—which features marine uniforms dating back to 1859 and photographs of marines in action during various conflicts around the world—will give you an understanding of the history and scope of the Marine Corps' role in defense of the United States.

Low Country girls are not unaware of the recruits on Parris Island. One story tells of a young woman who attended dances on the island and kept her eye on the unattached officers in search of husband material. Finding no suitable officer, she became engaged to an enlisted man. Before the wedding, however, an officer let her know he was interested in courting her, and she quickly rejected the enlisted man. It is doubtful if even Ann Landers could have helped her when she learned that the en-

152...

listed man had just inherited eighty-five thousand dollars.

Another story serves to illustrate the legendary closeness of the community of marines—and the power it conveys. After the Reverend C. B. Burns, the Methodist minister on Parris Island for sixteen years, preached his last sermon to the boys before being moved to a new pastorate, he was given a paper and told to "hand this to the bishop." When the bishop opened the paper, he found it to contain the names of 230 marines and officers requesting that the Reverend Burns be returned to his post. At that time, Methodist ministers were moved from a pastorate after four years, but with the United States Marine Corps guarding the reverend's back, the bishop was indeed moved to let him remain among the storied leathernecks of Parris Island.

Monument commemorating the marines who raised the flag on Iwo Jima's Mount Surabachi

PINCKNEY ISLAND

SOUTH CAROLINA

PINCKNEY ISLAND

Inhabited for some 10,000 years, Pinckney Island was known as Espalanga, Look-out, and Mackey's prior to about 1775. Alexander Mackey received two Proprietary grants for land on the island in 1710. Charles Pinckney later owned the island and willed it in 1769 to his son, Charles Cotesworth, who became a successful planter here.

ERECTED BY
BEAUFORT COUNTY HISTORICAL SOCIETY
1967

Pinckney Island marker

$\mathcal{P}$*inckney* $\mathcal{I}$*sland* is a small landmass off the mainland approach to Hilton Head Island. Skull Creek flows between Pinckney and Hilton Head.

Pinckney Island was known as Espalanga at some time during the Spanish pursuits. It was also known as Look-out Island and

Mackey Island, the latter in honor of Alexander Mackey, who received two land grants on the island in 1710.

In 1734, Charles Pinckney purchased Mackey Island and the four small islands nestled beside it. He changed the name to Pinckney Island. However, it would be generations before the first Pinckney lived there.

Pinckney was a London-educated lawyer, a legislator, a judge, and an adviser to the governor. He and his second wife, the former Eliza Lucas, had little time for Pinckney Island. They lived at Belmont Plantation on the Cooper River and kept a mansion in Charles Town. They also had considerable landholdings in England and sometimes spent several years at a time there. One of their primary interests was establishing fine libraries at their various residences. London booksellers kept them informed about the latest books. The Pinckneys read philosophy, political economy, and law. Although their libraries were stocked with novels, it is said they paid little attention to them.

Eliza Lucas Pinckney had another passion: botany. Her development of indigo cultivation has been noted in many volumes. After the fur trade fell off, indigo became for a time the most profitable commodity in the colony. By the end of the eighteenth century, it was an enormous part of South Carolina's commerce. Eliza also planted trees and gardens.

Charles Cotesworth Pinckney, the elder son of Charles and Eliza, was born in the family's Charles Town mansion in 1746. He was taken to England for his education in 1753. His father died in July 1758, while Charles Cotesworth Pinckney was still in England. According to his father's wishes, he was to inherit Pinckney Island and several other holdings at the age of twenty-one. Still, it would be years after that—the important years of our nation's founding—before he was in a position to give the island the attention it deserved.

Charles Cotesworth Pinckney was a well-educated lawyer by the time he returned to American soil. A graduate of Oxford University, he had been a student under Sir William Blackstone, author of the best-known history of English law. He set himself the task of rebuilding his father's law practice in Charles Town.

His marriage to Sally Middleton, daughter of Henry Middleton, in October 1773 was an event that merged two of the colony's most prominent families. By then, Pinckney had served in the provincial assembly, as the colony's attorney general, and in the provincial congress. He strongly favored separation from English rule.

Pinckney had a stellar Revolutionary War record. He was a captain in the first regiment of militia organized in South Carolina and was in command of Fort Johnson in 1775. Two years later, he fought in Pennsylvania with George Washington in the American defeats at Brandywine and Germantown. Later, he commanded Fort Moultrie during the siege of Charles Town and was taken prisoner when the British captured the city. Exchanged in 1782, he rejoined the Continental army and received a brevet promotion to brigadier general in 1783.

His wife died in 1784, leaving him with three small daughters. Two years later, he married Mary Stead.

In 1787, Pinckney was a delegate to the Constitutional Convention. But in the wake of the framing of the document that defines the United States of America, he showed himself reluctant to resume a full-time political career, declining President

Washington's offers of the lofty positions of secretary of war and secretary of state. Finally, in 1796, he accepted a post as minister to France, succeeding future president James Monroe. He was the Federalist candidate for the vice presidency in 1800.

It was in 1801 that he took up residence on Pinckney Island. But his political career was not quite over yet. In 1804, he was the Federalist Party candidate for president of the United States, winning fourteen electoral votes. He failed again in a bid for the presidency in 1808, when he captured forty-seven electoral votes.

Meanwhile, he and his wife built a graceful home in the most protected area of Pinckney Island, near a group of century-old trees. Mary set about equipping their house with what was recognized as one of the finest libraries in South Carolina. And Charles came to realize just how much like his mother he was. Growing things suddenly became his passion. For a quarter of a century, he built a large plantation labor force and enjoyed the life of a gentleman farmer. He planted exotic seeds from around the world and bred extraordinary strains of sheep, in addition to raising cattle, hogs, chickens, and horses. He died in 1825.

The mansion on Pinckney Island was noted throughout the area. Both home and garden were decorated with European statuary of great beauty. When the Church of the Cross Episcopal, one of the loveliest, most historic, and most photographed churches on the South Carolina coast, was completed in Bluffton, across the river from Pinckney Island, the Pinckney family wanted to make a donation to it. They sent over a handsome marble sundial from the garden on the island. The sundial's wide base, so high that it was reached by several steps, soon became a favorite among the children of Bluffton, who played upon it on summer afternoons.

The residents of Bluffton abandoned the village during the Civil War. When they returned, the base was gone and the sundial itself was half-buried in the sand at the foot of the bluff. No one has ever determined what happened to the base, but the sundial is now securely anchored on the church grounds.

Despite Charles Cotesworth Pinckney's efforts at building a solid, secure home in the most secure location he could find, the mansion on Pinckney Island was ultimately swept away in a hurricane.

In the twentieth century, Pinckney Island was bought by James Bruce of New York for use as a hunting island. Today, it has reverted to its natural state as the site of Pinckney Island National Wildlife Refuge.

The island is open to the public. Visitors may feel they have wandered onto the set of *Jurassic Park*—or at least into a greenhouse or an arboretum. The tropical foliage is so dense that one cannot see very far ahead on the curving road. Plants that look like swords and fans are crammed among leaves so large that they nearly block out the sun.

If Humpty Dumpty's wall had been located here, he'd never have hit the ground.

HILTON HEAD ISLAND

Harbour Town lighthouse

Skirting the Gulf Stream in 1521, Captain Pedro de Quexos of Spain sighted land at thirty-two degrees north latitude. Spanish Wells, a picturesque section of the island later known as Hilton Head, probably received its name because it was there that the Spanish ship replenished its supply of fresh water. Spanish Wells is still one of the most beautiful properties in South Carolina, a tropical paradise of palms, palmettos, private homes, and swimming pools.

The same island attracted the attention of Captain William Hilton on September 28, 1663. He wrote, "The ayr is clear and sweet, the Countrey very pleasant and delightful." Although he didn't give the island a name, it was shown on subsequent English maps as Hilton Head.

It was not the English but the Irish who were first granted land on the island. Hilton Head was included in a forty-thousand-acre grant to John Bayley "of Ballinclough of the County of Tipperary" on August 16, 1698. Other men of Irish birth who obtained land on the island were Tuscarora Jack Barnwell of Port Royal; John Talbot, whose name was written *Tailbird* on the deed; and John Hanahan, whom the locals called "Honeyhorn."

The planters on Hilton Head Island supported the American cause in the Revolutionary War, while their neighbors on Daufuskie Island were largely Tory in their sympathies. Indigo was the chief money crop in those years. Independence brought an end to the English subsidy on indigo, after which cotton took its place of supremacy.

William Elliott seems to have been the first Hilton Head planter to raise sea-island cotton. In 1791, John Screven planted thirty or forty acres, after which cotton planting spread rapidly. The English market welcomed it. Though there were only a few plantations on the island, Hilton Head's twenty-five thousand acres were at one time one of the most productive cotton-growing areas on all of South Carolina's sea islands.

Some of the most popular Hilton Head stories concern planter William Eddings Baynard, born in 1800. By the age of twenty, Baynard had already been bequeathed the 600-acre Spanish Wells Plantation and the adjoining 850-acre Muddy Creek Plantation on Hilton Head. However, he wanted to acquire beautiful Braddocks Point Plantation, the prime property on the island. The ruins of this plantation can be seen today at Sea Pines Plantation near the intersection of Baynard Park Road and Plantation Drive.

Baynard had one problem. Braddocks Point was owned by his neighbor and friend Captain Jack Stoney. In 1830, at a meeting of the cotton planters, Baynard suggested the men put up their plantations as stakes in a game of poker. The idea didn't sit well with Stoney, but Baynard insisted. Rather than back away from a test of honor, Stoney finally agreed to the stakes. When the game was over, Baynard had won Braddocks Point and its thousand acres of land.

Baynard was thus firmly situated as a planter, his cotton commanding a top price of twelve dollars a pound. He was a man on whom many a young woman set her sights.

Ruins of Baynard Hall

When he was ready for marriage, Baynard selected a Savannah belle. He put the finishing touches on Baynard Hall, a new home at Braddocks Point, before heading to Savannah for the wedding. Unfortunately, Savannah was in the throes of a yellow-fever epidemic. Baynard hurriedly got his bride aboard a vessel and made for Hilton Head. While on the boat, the young woman showed symptoms of the dreaded fever. When the boat docked at Braddocks Point, the groom carried his weak bride to Baynard Hall. She died during her first night at her new home.

It was for this young wife that Baynard built a mausoleum outfitted with twenty-one crypts and a heavy oak door; the mausoleum was located adjacent to the Zion Chapel of Ease at what is now the intersection of William Hilton Parkway and Matthews Drive. The young woman was laid to rest in a pine coffin made in the shape of her body. The coffin was then placed in a black carriage draped in black crepe, as was the custom of the time. Pulled

Zion Chapel of Ease

by four matching black horses, the carriage began its long, slow ride to the mausoleum. Baynard laid his wife to rest in a crypt and dictated that the door never be closed.

Baynard later remarried and had two sons by his second wife. He died of yellow fever in 1849 and was buried in the same fashion as his first wife.

Shortly after his burial, people on Hilton Head reported witnessing a ghostly carriage pulled by four black horses. On moonlit nights, it could be seen winding its way down the road from Baynard Hall to the mausoleum. Inside the carriage, prostrated by grief, a man sat and moaned out his love for his departed wife. The ride was a long one—about ten miles. As the coach neared the crypt, it faded away right before the eyes of those brave enough to watch. Many believed the apparition was the ghost of William Baynard, who had never fully accepted the loss of his first wife.

In recent years, Hilton Head developer Joe Fraser was in charge of laying out a road past the old mausoleum. Some expensive building materials and equipment were left there, and Fraser sent two men to guard them. As they sat sleepily at their post, the men noticed a carriage decked out for a funeral being drawn by four black horses. The men fled the scene.

The next night, Fraser ordered them to return to the site. They agreed to give it another try. One of them carried a pistol. When the black carriage came down the road again, he fired toward it. The carriage disappeared. Fraser's men refused to act as night watchmen ever again.

Early in the Civil War, Union war chiefs decided their blockading vessels needed a base on the southern portion of the Atlantic coast. On November 7, 1861, a fifty-vessel flotilla under Commodore Samuel F. DuPont overran Fort Walker, a Confederate installation on Hilton Head. In one of the many ironies of the war, Confederate brigadier general Thomas F. Drayton found himself defending the island while Union captain Percival Drayton of the *Pocohontas* attacked it. Both brothers had grown up on Fish Hall Plantation on Hilton Head.

Fort Walker fell to the Federals and was renamed Fort Welles. It was actually Union occupying forces who established the first town on Hilton Head. They called it Port Royal. Its citizens supported a garrison of twenty-five thousand to thirty thousand troops, as well as ships of the blockading squadron. Port Royal had its own post office, stores, newspapers, sawmills, hotels, and theaters. By May 1862, a customs house was established, and the town was declared open to foreign trade.

At some point during the war, an experimental steam-gun emplacement was located at the fort. It was discarded after test firings, but not before one of its shells started a disastrous forest fire on a nearby island.

Today, the concrete foundation of the steam cannon and the earthen mounds of the fort are still visible, but no traces of the old town of Port Royal are to be found.

The Union takeover of Hilton Head marked the beginning of the end of the production of sea-island cotton. As on South Carolina's other sea islands, families fled their plantations. Knowing little about local agriculture, Federal soldiers sent the entire crop of 1861 north to be ginned without retaining the best seeds for next year's planting. Cotton prices plummeted to sixty-six cents a pound by 1866 and to four cents a pound by 1890. The boll weevil invasion in 1919 destroyed the last of the splendid crop that had made millionaires of antebellum planters like the Baynards. Though the Baynard family was able to reclaim much of its land for taxes after the war, it never regained its status. Its manor house was soon overgrown with the vines and thick undergrowth typical of the island region.

When General William T. Sherman completed his March to the Sea on January 16, 1865, he issued a field order setting aside the sea islands and a band of territory reaching thirty miles inland for the sole use of freed slaves. Thousands of them flocked to Beaufort to take advantage of the lands, which they initially believed were to be given them.

Most freedmen ended up buying land with money made from labor on the plantations, which were operated by Northern agents appointed by the government. Some former slaves claimed land on the plantations where they had been born, moving their cabins from the old slave "street" to their new property. However, they did not actually gain title to their land until Congress ordered an amendment to the Freedman's Bureau Act of July 16, 1866, at which time most public lands were sold "to such persons and to such only as have acquired and are now occupying lands under and agreeably to the provisions of General Sherman's special field order."

The injustice of these sales soon became apparent. Under the Redemption Act of 1872, former owners were permitted to buy the lands still in possession of the government upon payment of taxes, costs, interest, and penalties. And so the social experiment ended.

Two events stand out in the history of Hilton Head Island.

Former slaves used to approximate their age from the time "when gun shoot," meaning the firing of the guns at Fort Walker during the Civil War. The other landmark event was the hurricane of Friday, October 13, 1893, when many people lost their lives and much property was destroyed. All of Hilton Head was under water. If the Civil War failed to bring the island to its knees, the hurricane of 1893 did.

Toward the end of the century, some former slaves sold their property to wealthy Northerners for use as hunting preserves. But the greater portion of Hilton Head was still in the hands of plantation owners when W. P. Clyde of the Clyde Line steamship company began acquiring Hilton Head land. Of the five thousand acres not in his holdings, a tract of about eighteen hundred acres was owned by the North Carolina Hunting Club, a tract of about five hundred acres was owned by Harriet Gonzales, and the remainder—between two and three thousand acres—was owned in small plots by six hundred former slaves. Roy L. Rainey and W. L. Hurley acquired the Clyde property in 1918 and soon sold it to brothers-in-law Landon K. Thorne and Alfred Loomis of New York. Thorne and Loomis thus came into possession of about twenty thousand of Hilton Head's twenty-five thousand acres.

The Thorne and Loomis families renovated a house that had been under construction when the Civil War broke out and was somehow left standing when the Yankees departed the island. The families lived together in the attractive, comfortable house when they came for the winter hunting season. Situated in a large grove of cedar trees, the house sat near a smaller cottage. Just across the road were barns and dog kennels, along with cottages occupied by employees of the estate. On a more isolated part of the island was an English-style hunting lodge. It boasted a balcony enclosing the second story and a massive fireplace at the end of a huge hall. The lodge served as living quarters for the caretaker of the estate.

One of Thorne and Loomis's pet projects was the construction of four hundred acres of duck ponds. Three thousand or more ducks were turned loose into the ponds for breeding purposes. The ponds eventually furnished the best duck shooting anywhere in this section of the country. Other game—particularly deer and quail—was plentiful on the island. There were also wild boars, descendants of once-domesticated animals.

Probably the greatest surprise strangers got when they stepped onto the island was the number of smart automobiles in residence. Indeed, the sophisticated Northerners and their guests rode the serpentine, sandy island roads in style. And there was no need to buy license tags, as nobody kept up the roads.

Among visitors' favorite sites on the island were the small cemeteries deep in the woods where slave descendants buried their dead. There, one found graves decorated with lampshades, medicine bottles, milk bottles, dishes, bells, spectacles, coffee pots, and shells of every conceivable shape and design. Such objects were placed on the graves because they were the last things used by the deceased person. It was believed that if relatives placed the items on a grave, the collection would prevent the spirit of the dead from returning to earth.

In those days, Hilton Head Island and Jenkins Island were

connected by a causeway and considered almost the same island. The Hilton Head post office was actually located on 250-acre Jenkins Island, the point of embarkation for both islands. It was there that the steamer *Clivedon* of the Beaufort-Savannah line stopped on its trips three times a week. The boat was the only means of communication with the outside world except for the radio and telephone in the island's lighthouse and the telephone in the house of J. E. Lawrence, the superintendent of the Thorne and Loomis estate.

Lawrence was sometimes called the "dictator" of Hilton Head Island, although he disliked that sobriquet. He came to Hilton Head in 1892 to work in one of the island's stores. He left for a few years, then was lured back in 1903 to accept the position as superintendent of W. P. Clyde's estate. Lawrence saw former slaves leave the island, until there were only a handful remaining. They farmed little but had vivid memories of the Civil War. One of them claimed to have been present when Jefferson Davis was brought to Hilton Head Island and put aboard a ship.

In his position as superintendent for Thorne and Loomis, Lawrence oversaw fifteen employees, looked after school matters, attended to the roads when they became impassable, and was the island's police force, although he had little to do in that regard.

Beaufort newspaper reporter Chlotilde Martin summarized the influence of—and local residents' feelings toward—wealthy Northerners like Thorne and Loomis who came south and bought up land for sporting use:

The property which was once destroyed by alien hands is being restored, and by the descendants of the destroyers. There are probably more northern landowners in Beaufort County than in any of the other coastal counties of the states. They have built hunting clubs and palatial homes. In those rare instances where the original plantation homes remained, they have been restored to their former graciousness. Some of the new owners, sensing the fitness of things, have reconstructed old homes where none remained, with the aid of photographs in the hands of the former owners. While the majority of these new owners come down only for the hunting season, a few of them have become citizens of South Carolina and remain on their plantations here the year around, finding the mild, even climate more to their liking than the cold of the North. Few of them plant the plantations, although one or two raise cattle as a hobby. Several of the old plantations are owned by men from Georgia, who bought the lands for timber or cattle raising, but with these few exceptions, the new ownerships have taken more than 100,000 of the 300,000 taxable acres of this county out of cultivation.

A syndicate of Southerners bought the island in 1950 to harvest its bountiful timber crop. Six years later, Charles Fraser, son of the head of the syndicate, purchased land from his father and set about preserving the southern end of the island. A World War II veteran and law-school graduate, Fraser had worked three years for the Augusta, Georgia, law firm that handled the affairs of Augusta National Golf Club. When he looked at Hilton Head, he was more inclined to see the natural beauty first witnessed by Captain Pedro de Quexos and Captain William Hilton than he was to see the dollar signs of a timber business. He had a dream about the possibilities of the tropical island.

Fraser engaged the services of Harvard-educated land planner Hideo Sasaki, whose master plan for the project won the Certificate of Excellence from the American Society of Landscape Architects. Sea Pines Plantation was the glorious result.

"We didn't cut any of the virgin pine forest along the ocean," Fraser said. "We didn't cut any hardwoods, so all the live oaks, the magnolias, all of that survived. Then we set aside 14,000 acres of parks and forests here, not counting golf courses. Making this a permanent park while at the same time making it a human settlement was what we accomplished."

By 1956, the James F. Byrnes Memorial Bridge linked Hilton Head with the mainland. The first golf course on the island was completed in 1959. The eighteen-hole Ocean Course is one of the most photographed in America. Harbour Town, where huge yachts ride at anchor near the lighthouse, is a must for dining, shopping, or just relaxing in a rocking chair and looking across Calibogue Sound toward Daufuskie Island.

Charles Fraser prides himself on his knowledge of Hilton Head's twenty-two golf courses, some of which are among the best in America. Fraser is a part of that history, although he cannot play a lick.

Despite its reputation as a not-to-be-missed vacation, retirement, shopping, and recreational area, much of Hilton Head is reminiscent of the age of the sea-island cotton plantations. Golf courses, tennis courts, gracious homes, marinas, and resort hotels fit comfortably into the tangled jungle of tall pines, moss-draped live oaks, magnolias, palmettos, and bay trees. The tabby ruins of Baynard Hall can still be seen on the island. And although Fort Walker is crumbling, two miles of the original fortifications remain within Port Royal Plantation.

DAUFUSKIE ISLAND

Daufuskie Island is about six and a half miles long and three miles wide. It is bounded on the southeast by the Atlantic Ocean, on the northeast by Calibogue Sound, on the northwest and west by the Cooper River, on the west by Ramshorn Creek, on the southwest by the New River, and on the south by the Mongin River. Although Daufuskie's elevation is greater than that of most other islands in the area, its highest point is only thirty feet above sea level. It is the state's southernmost barrier island. A mile to the east, Hilton Head holds forth. Fourteen miles to the west, Savannah reigns.

The island's name has known many spellings, among them Dawfoskee, D'Awfoskee, and Da-fus-key. Some people believe the name came about because the island is "the first key" to entering the Savannah River. As in the days of the Indians, no bridge connects the island to the mainland. People and commodities are delivered by boat or by air.

Daufuskie Island was granted to Captain John Mongin by King George II in 1740. During the violent Yemassee Indian massacres that century, the area of the island still known as Bloody Point received its name. Indeed, the Indians knew the entire island as the "Place of Blood."

During the Revolutionary War, Daufuskie residents supported the British cause, a loyalty that drew the wrath of neighboring islands. The following excerpt from the January 30, 1782, edition of the *Royal Gazette* of Charles Town describes a horrible incident that resulted: "We are informed from Savannah, that about Christmas last, a gang of banditti came to a house on Daufusky Island, where Capt. Martinangel of the Royal Militia was lying sick, and whilst two of them held his wife, another, named Israel Andrews, shot him dead; they afterwards plundered Mrs. Martinangel and her children of almost everything they had. These wretches came from Hilton Head Island; they stile themselves the Bloody Legion."

Many years after the Martinangels were laid to rest, vandals broke into a crypt, opened their coffins, stole whatever personal items they found, and left without closing the coffins. Years later, the coffins were broken into again. This time, the vandals were in for a surprise, as a large snake uncoiled from inside one of the coffins.

On April 9, 1983, the Hilton Head Historical Society placed a historical marker in Mary Dunn Cemetery on Daufuskie Island in memory of Captain Philip Martinangel. In that cemetery are two long, narrow cast-iron coffins that are believed to contain the remains of Martinangel and his wife. An unusual feature of the coffins is the glass windows placed directly over the faces of the deceased.

Among the first wealthy landowners on Daufuskie were furrier and trapper George Haig, the Blodgett family, Squire Pope, and John Mongin. The grandest and most elaborate plantation home was Melrose, built in 1848. After John Mongin's granddaughter married her tutor, John Stoddard, and honeymooned at Melrose Abbey in Scotland, the couple sailed back to Daufuskie and designed a home after its Scottish namesake. Included in the plantation's seven hundred acres were an avenue of oaks leading to the mansion and five acres of formal rose gardens, which proved a popular place to entertain. Wealthy planter families from Savannah like the famous Noble Jones clan rode to Daufuskie in a steamer and picnicked in the rose gardens.

By the Civil War, six other sea-island cotton plantations had been carved out of the Daufuskie wilderness. When General William T. Sherman ordered Captain John Monroe's regiment to burn the island's mansions in 1862, Monroe chose to protect Melrose. He said he had never seen a place so lovely, noting in his diary the beauty of the roses, the walkways, the trees, and the mansion itself. Melrose ultimately succumbed to fire anyway, in 1912.

Union Baptist Church, built around 1863, is still in use, right down to the kerosene chandeliers. The church was constructed with two doors entering the sanctuary, one for men and the other for women and children. Today, a mainland minister comes to the island every other week to hold services. It is said that the

Union Baptist Church

church is always full by eleven-thirty. However, the service starts at eleven! Such is "island time," according to which it is always fitting to be thirty minutes late. People on Daufuskie seem to live their lives at a slower pace.

Two lighthouses were built on Daufuskie in the mid-1870s. Haig Point Lighthouse was constructed facing Hilton Head Island and Bloody Point Lighthouse facing Savannah. Both beacons were fueled by kerosene. Ships lined up the two lights in order to get their bearings.

Haig Point Lighthouse is believed to be haunted. Residents say they have witnessed a ghost in the light, a woman they call Maggie or "the Ghost of the Black Lady." She can supposedly be seen from water or land.

Bloody Point Lighthouse was moved in 1910 because of erosion. It stands about a mile from its original location. Both lighthouses were shut down during World War II.

Daufuskie had two thousand inhabitants at the beginning of the twentieth century. The coming of the boll weevil in 1919 struck a blow to the planters as devastating as the Civil War. The island's economy was revived for a time by truck farming and logging. During the 1920s, a narrow-gauge logging train ran from one end of the island to the other, transporting timber to a dock on the river.

"Eighty percent of the islanders worked in oysters" toward the middle of the century, according to Bob Burn, a native of Daufuskie. Oysters were sold in Bluffton, after which the shells were hauled back and piled along the Daufuskie shore, where they served as a sea wall. Oystering was a profitable enterprise from World War II until 1959, when scientists deemed the water polluted and the oysters unfit for consumption. At the height of oystering on Daufuskie, everyone on the island who wanted a job had one. But following the reports of pollution, nobody had a job.

Mary Field Elementary School was based at Union Baptist Church on Daufuskie until a new schoolhouse was constructed in 1936. This humble school's claim to fame is a teacher who has since become a best-selling legend in the literary world.

In 1969, Pat Conroy replaced Frances Jones, who had lived on the island all her life and had begun teaching school at the age of fifteen. Conroy taught in one room of the two-room schoolhouse, and the late Julia Sanders Johnson taught in the other. As South Carolina elementary schools were required to have a principal, Johnson also filled that role.

Many of Conroy's students on Daufuskie had only occasional contact with the mainland. His experience in upsetting the Beau-

Mary Field Elementary School

fort County School Board with his unorthodox teaching methods provided the material with which he launched his writing career. Although Conroy is not a South Carolina native, he is a "local" writer in the sense that most of his books are set in the Charleston-Beaufort area. *The Water Is Wide* is his book about his year of teaching on Daufuskie. It was made into the successful movie *Conrack*. Conroy has since written such acclaimed works as *The Great Santini, The Lords of Discipline, The Prince of Tides*, and *Beach Music*. He is less well remembered for his performance as Scrooge in Mount Carmel Church's production of *A Christmas Carol*, presented during his tenure at the school.

Mary Field was the oldest public school in Beaufort County until it was replaced by the new Daufuskie Island Elementary School in the mid-1990s.

Today, Daufuskie is an intriguing mix of the spectacular and the humble. Three of the island's original seven plantations—Melrose, Bloody Point, and Haig Point—have been developed. The others have proven resistant to change for the simple reason that there is no clear deed to the property.

The opening of Haig Point and Melrose Plantations as residential and golfing communities led to an increase in population on the island. The International Paper Company bought Haig Point and Melrose in 1984.

The exclusive Haig Point resort community is stunning. Its residents enjoy private ferry service to and from the mainland, but they rarely have cause to leave a place where they can swim, ride horseback, and play golf and tennis to their heart's content.

The comfortable Strachan Mansion, which serves as the clubhouse at Haig Point, was once the vacation home of the Strachan family on St. Simons Island, Georgia. It fell into disrepair and was scheduled for demolition, only to have the International Paper Company come to the rescue when it was discovered what a terrific bargain the home was. The purchase price was only a dollar!

International Paper arranged to float the mansion on a barge a hundred miles up the Intracoastal Waterway to Daufuskie. The engineering task was a giant one. Network television crews were on hand to film the mansion as it squeezed under low bridges and sat in the mud waiting for the tide to rise. Though the move was successful, the new owners didn't realize quite the bargain they'd anticipated. They may have paid only a dollar for the mansion, but it cost them nearly a million to move it!

Jack Nicklaus designed the course at Melrose Golf Club. No

trucks or cars are allowed there, but then again, they're not really needed.

It may surprise first-time visitors to learn that, except for the spectacular developments at Haig Point and Melrose and a few other small residential areas, the typical Daufuskie house still has a front porch, a chicken house, and a shade tree and sits on a dirt road. For many years, some islanders have gotten around in a cart pulled by an ox. These residents could hardly be more different from their well-to-do neighbors.

One such old-time resident was Sarah Hudson Grant, a midwife who birthed over a hundred children. When her husband, an undertaker, died, she took over his job as well. As the islanders said, "Sarah bring 'em and she take 'em away."

Another popular couple was the W. W. Scoutens, who took such pride in the ancient Indian mortar and pestle they discovered intact among all the Indian pottery, beads, and other relics on the

Haig Point lighthouse

island that they set them at their front steps, where they attracted the attention of all who entered the house.

The Mongin name has been prominent on the island for generations. Today, it is worn by the descendants of slaves on what was once the plantation of David Mongin. The descendants still retain the name they were forced to take in a time long before country clubs came to Daufuskie.

These longtime residents never want to leave their island. As one man put it, "I wouldn't trade a teaspoon of Daufuskie for the rest of the state of South Carolina."

Bibliography

I did the predominant part of my research for this book in the Works Progress Administration files at the Caroliniana Library in Columbia, South Carolina, and the Library of Congress in Washington, D.C. Many of the writers who lived on the coast of South Carolina during the 1930s worked for the WPA recording interviews. I never start writing a book without consulting the WPA files.

Able, E. Eugene. "Daufuskie Island." *Sandlapper* (December 1973): 19–24.

Alpert, Hollis. *The Life and Times of Porgy and Bess*. New York: Alfred A. Knopf, 1990.

Baxley, Bennett, ed. *St. James–Santee Parish Historical Sketches*. St. James–Santee Parish Historical Society, 1995.

Black, J. Gary. *My Friend the Gullah*. Columbia, S.C.: R. L. Bryan Company, 1974.

Burn, Billie. *Stirrin' the Pots on Daufuskie*. Spartanburg, S.C.: Reprint Company, 1995.

Christophersen, Merrill G. *Biography of an Island: General C. C. Pinckney's Sea Island Plantation*. Sennimore, Wis.: Westbury Associates, 1976.

Cooper, Gail. "The Nine Old Houses of Pawleys Island." *Sandlapper* (Spring 1997): 29–33.

Dabbs, Edith M. *Sea Island Diary: A History of St. Helena Island*. Spartanburg, S.C.: Reprint Company, 1983.

Ewen, David. *A Journey to Greatness: The Life and Music of George Gershwin*. New York: Henry Holt, 1956.

Glen, Isabella C. *Life on St. Helena Island*. New York: Carlton Press, 1980.

Gordon, Kay. "The Lure of an Unbridged Isle." *Sandlapper* (March-April 1990): 65–72.

Graydon, Nell S. *Tales of Beaufort*. Columbia, S.C.: R. L. Bryan Company, 1985.

Green, Ron. "The Man Who Doesn't Play Golf." *Carolina Fairways* (Fall 1996): 46–47.

Hamrick, Tom. "You Can Lead a House to Water." *Sandlapper* (August 1970): 30–32.

Iseley, N. Jane. *Plantations of the Low Country of South Carolina, 1697–1865*. Greensboro, N.C.: Legacy Publications, 1985.

Johnson, Clint. *Civil War Blunders*. Winston-Salem, N.C.: John F. Blair, Publisher, 1997.

————. *Touring the Carolinas' Civil War Sites*. Winston-Salem, N.C.: John F. Blair, Publisher, 1996.

Linder, Suzanne C. *Atlas of Rice Plantations of the ACE Basin*. Columbia, S.C.: South Carolina Department of Archives and History, 1996.

MacDowell, Dorothy K. "Beaufort County." *South Carolina Magazine* (June 1970): 11–15.

Prevost, Charlotte Kaminski, and Effie Leland Wilder. *Pawleys Island: A Living Legend*. Columbia, S.C.: The State Printing Company, 1972.

Pringle, Elizabeth Allston. *Chronicles of Chicora Wood*. New York: Scribner's, 1922.

Puckette, Clara Childs. *Edisto: A Sea Island Principality*. Cleveland, Ohio: Seaforth Publications.

—————. "Edisto Island 1865." *Sandlapper* (March 1975): 29–33, 36.

Rhyne, Nancy. *Touring the Coastal South Carolina Backroads*. Winston-Salem, N.C.: John F. Blair, Publisher, 1992.

Rogers, Aida. "Tastiest Tea in North America." *Sandlapper* (Autumn 1993): 30–34.

Rogers, George C., Jr. *History of Beaufort County*. Columbia, S.C.: University of South Carolina Press, 1997.

Rutledge, Archibald. "I've Watched Some Great Escapes." *South Carolina Magazine* (November 1957): 9–10.

Smith, Alice R. Huger, and D. E. Huger. *The Dwelling Houses of Charleston*. New York, Diadem Books, 1917.

Stoney, Samuel Galliard. *Plantations of the South Carolina Low Country*. Charleston, S.C.: Carolina Arts Association, 1939.

Taylor, W. M. "Hilton Head Island: Emerald of the Carolinian Coast." *South Carolina Magazine* (April 1967): 32–34.

Tom Yawkey Wildlife Center. Columbia, S.C.: South Carolina Department of Natural Resources, 1979.

Twining, Mary A., and Keith Baird, eds. *Sea Island Roots: The African Presence in South Carolina and Georgia*. Trenton, N.J.: Africa World Press, 1991.

Yarbrough, Frances C. "Porgy and Bess." *Sandlapper* (July 1969): 77–79.

Young, Claiborne S. *Cruising Guide to Coastal South Carolina and Georgia*. 3rd ed. Winston-Salem, N.C.: John F. Blair, Publisher, 1996.

Index

Adventure, 103

Agnes (ghost), 95

Alexander, Edward Porter, 25

All Saints Episcopal Church, 11

All Saints Summer Parsonage, 18

Allston House, 18

Allston, J. Motte, 9

Allston, Robert Francis Withers, 14, 16

American Classic Tea, 79

Anderson, Robert, 52, 55, 56, 60

Angel, Justis, 75

Angel, Martha Waight, 75

Angel Oak, 75–77

Ashley River, 61, 87

Astor, Mrs. William Backhouse, Jr., 96

Ayllon, Lucas Vasquez de, 131

Ball, John, 60

Barnes, Fred J., 137

Barnwell, Edward, 95, 96

Barnwell, Margaret Manigault, 95, 96

Barnwell, Robert, 73

Barnwell, Stephen Elliott, 96

Bay Point Island, 141

Bayley, John, 160

Baynard, Ephraim Mikell, 104

Baynard Hall, 162, 163, 171

Baynard, William Edings, 160–63

Beach Music, 177

Beaufort, 4, 116, 127, 132, 133, 136

Beaufort County, 142, 169, 177

Beaufort County School Board, 176

Beaufort-Savannah Line, 168

Beauregard, P. G. T., 55, 60, 88

Belmont Plantation, 155

Berkeley County, 13

Bermuda Island, S.C., 129

Bethlehem A.M.E. Church, 96

Big Apple Club, 46

Big Apple (dance), 19, 46

Big Goat Island, 44

Black River, 33, 35

Blackbeard. *See* Teach, Edward

Blackstone, William, 156

Blaisdell, Nicholas, 116

Blake, James Pierpont, 116

Bleak Hall, 123

Blessing, 59

Bliss, Emily, 116

Blodgett family, 174

Bloody Legion, 173

Bloody Point, 173, 178

Bloody Point Lighthouse, 175

Bluffton, 157, 158, 176

Bohicket Creek, 82, 84, 86

Bohicket Indian village, 86

boll weevil, 5, 63, 88, 117, 165, 176

Bonnet, Stede, 8, 49, 50

"boo-daddies," 112

Boston Red Sox, 26, 32, 36, 37

Botkin, Henry, 65

Braddocks Point Plantation, 161, 162
Brick Baptist Church, 133
Brick House, 107, 108, 114, 123
Brickyard Plantation, 124
Bruce, James, 158
Bull family, 39
Bull, William, 131
Bulls Bay, 39
Bulls Harbor, 38
Bulls Island, 38–43
Burden, Mrs. Kinsey, 2
Burden's Island, 4
Burn, Bob, 176
Burns, C. B., 153
Buzzard, Dr., 137, 138
Buzzard's Island, 129

Caines, Sawney, 25
Calibogue Sound, 170, 172
California Plantation, 116
Cameron, J. M., 138
Campsen, George E., Jr., 43
Canterbury, archbishop of, 35
Cape Island, 41
Cape Romain National Wildlife Refuge, 41, 43
Capers Island, 141
Carolina Yacht Club, 82
Carter, Jimmy, 135
Casamar, 18
Cassina Point, 113, 115, 123
Castle Pinckney, 54, 55
Cat Island, 21, 25, 26, 27, 29, 33–37
Chaplin, Eliza H., 135
Chaplin family, 131, 132

Chaplin, John, 124, 125
Chaplin, Tom B., 132
Charles Town. *See* Charleston
Charles Town Landing, 86
Charlesfort, 148, 149, 150
Charleston, 50, 56, 57, 76, 106–7, 109, 156
Charleston Battery, 57
Charleston County, 46, 68, 127
Charleston Harbor, 57, 114
Charleston Naval Base, 60, 61
Charleston Seashore and Railroad Company, 45
Charleston Tea Plantation, 78, 79, 81
Chisolm Island, 129
chukars, 98
Church, Henry F., 64
Church of the Cross Episcopal, 157
Civil War: and Daufuskie Island, 174; and Edisto Island, 108, 110, 114–17; and Fort Sumter, 52, 55–57; and Hilton Head Island, 163, 164; and James Island, 66, 67; and Kiawah Island, 88; and Pinckney Island, 158; and St. Helena Island, 134–36; and Yonges Island, 94
Clark, Ephraim, 104
Cleveland, Grover, 25
Clivedon, 168
Club House Island, 44
Clyde, W. P., 166, 168
Cobb, Ty, 26
Coffin, Ebenezer, 131
Coffin family, 131
Coffin Point Plantation, 130, 131, 138

College of Charleston, 60, 61, 104, 105, 149

Collins, Alexander, 38

Collins family, 39

Collins, John, 38

Collins, Jonah, 38

Colony Gardens, 126

Combahee River, 99

Conrack, 177

Conroy, Pat, 147, 176, 177

Cooper River, 60, 61, 172

Corner Plantation, 133

Cove Inlet, 45

Curley Hut, 96–97, 99, 100

Cuthbert Point, 127

Daniels, Jeff, 33

Dataw Island, 129

Daufuskie Elementary School, 177

Daufuskie Island, 160, 170, 172–80

Davis, Jefferson, 168

DeBry, Theodore, 149

DeKalb, Baron, 22

Dodge, Donald D., 123

Dominick, Gayer B., 40

Dominick House, 40

Drayton, John, 74

Drayton, Percival, 164

Drayton, Thomas, 164

Drunken Jack Island, 7–12

Dryer, Eileen, 100

Dryer, G. Herman, 100

Dunlap, William, 103, 104

DuPont, Samuel F., 164

Eden, Charles, 145

Edingsville Beach, 110

Edisto Island, 102–23, 132

Edisto Island Baptist Church, 110

Edisto Island Presbyterian Church, 110, 117

Edisto River, 85, 101, 103, 120

Edistow Indians, 102, 103

Egg Island, 130

Eggbank Island. *See* Egg Island

Elliott, William, 2, 93, 160

Enoch Dean, 94

Espalanga. *See* Pinckney Island

Estherville Plantation, 23

Fairly, John L., 139

Fenwick, Edward, 72

Fenwick Hall, 72, 77

Fenwick Island. *See* Johns Island

Fenwick, John, 72

Fenwick, Thomas, 73

First United States Artillery, 55

Fish Hall Plantation, 164

FitzSimons, Christopher, 95

FitzSimons, Mrs. Christopher, 95

Five Fathom Creek, 39

Flagg, Arthur, Jr., 11

Flagg, Arthur, Sr., 10, 11

Flagg, Georgeanna, 11

Flagg, J. Ward, 10, 11

"Flagg Storm, the," 12

Fleming, Mack, 79

Fly Away Home, 33

Folly Beach, 64–68

Folly Island, 57, 64

Fort Fremont, 137

Fort Johnson, 55, 60, 156

Fort Moultrie, 51, 52, 54, 55, 156

Fort San Felipe, 149

Fort San Marcos, 149

Fort Sumter, 52, 54, 55, 56, 57, 60, 66, 81, 88

Fort Walker, 164, 166, 171

Fort Welles, 164

Fraser, Charles, 169, 170

Fraser, Joe, 163

Freedman's Bureau Act, 165

Fripp, Edgar, 132, 136

Fripp family, 132

Fripp Inlet, 142

Fripp Island, 131, 141, 144–47

Fripp, John, 131, 144, 145

Fripp, Sarah, 132

Frogmore, 137

Frogmore Plantation, 131

Frogmore Stew, 138

George II, 44, 139, 144, 173

Georgetown, 21–23, 34

Georgetown Light, 24

Georgetown Rifle Guards, 29

Gershwin, George, 64–66, 89

"Ghost of the Black Lady, the," 175

Gibbes, Mary, 87

Gibson, Jim, 30

Gilling, Arthur Alfred, 110

"Gold Bug, The," 52

Gonzales, Harriet, 166

Gordillo, Francisco, 131

Grant, Cary, 98

Grant, Sarah Hudson, 179

Gray Man, 19–20

Grayson, William J., 131

Great Santini, The, 177

Green, Charles, 119

Green, Jack, 8

Green, Phyllis, 59

Grimball family, 103

Grimball, Paul, 103, 104

Grimball, William H., 82, 83

Gullah, 4–5, 65, 77

Hagley Plantation, 15

"hags," 58, 112

Haig, George, 174

Haig Point Lighthouse, 175

Haig Point resort, 178, 179

Hall, William Barclay, 79

Hamilton, Paul, 107

Hamilton, Paul, III, 107

Hampton Plantation, 40, 41

Hampton, Wade, 139

Hanahan, John "Honeyhorn," 160

"hants," 58, 112

Harbour Town, 170

Harley, R. K., 126

Haskell, William H., 83

Haugwitz-Reventlow, Count, 98

Heyward, DuBose, 64, 65

Heywood, Maria, 12

Hibben's Ferry, 45

Hiller, Jean Hollander. *See* Yawkey, Jean Hollander Hiller

Hilton Head Historical Society, 173

Hilton Head Island, 2, 134, 154, 159–73, 175

Hilton, William, 103, 131, 160, 170

Hinson, William G., 61

Hoban, James, 109

Hog Island, 129

Hollings, Ernest F., 47

Hollings, Peatsy, 46

Holtzman, Richard M., 101

Hopkinson, Carolina de Lafayette Seabrook, 109, 115

Hopkinson, Francis, 109

Hopkinson, James, 109

Horry, Ben, 11

Horse Island, 129

Hot and Hot Fish Club, 8–10, 11

Huger, Benjamin, 22

Huger, Francis Kinloch, 22

Hume, Alexander, 35

Hume Plantation, 35

"Hungry Necks," 49

Hunting Island, 141–43, 146, 147

Hunting Island State Park, 141–43

"Hunting Islands, the," 141

Huntington Beach State Park, 7, 12

Hurley, W. L., 166

Hurricane Hugo, 18, 20, 46

Hutton, Barbara, 98

Hutton, E. F., 96, 99

Hutton, Franklyn L., 96, 98, 99

Hutton, Irene Curley, 99

"Independent Republic of Edisto Island, the," 114

Indian Hill, 130

Indiana, 150

International Paper Company, 178

Intracoastal Waterway, 84, 178

Island Cat, 43

Isle of Palms, 44–47, 68

Jacque (pirate), 8

James F. Byrnes Memorial Bridge, 170

James, George S., 55

James Island, 55, 58–60, 61–66, 67

James Island Agricultural Society, 61, 63

James Island Presbyterian Church, 64

James Towne, 60. *See also* New Towne

James Whaley Plantation, 116

Jasper, William, 51

Jenkins, Benjamin, 80, 108

Jenkins, Benjamin, Jr., 80

Jenkins family, 108

Jenkins Island, 167, 168

Jenkins, Joseph, 108, 114

Jenkins, Samuel, 80

Jenkins, W. Reynolds, 82

"Jim Island boys," 82

John Adams, 94

Johns Island, 1–2, 69–77, 89, 93

Johns Island Presbyterian Church, 69, 70

Johnson, Julia Sanders, 176

Johnston, Sarah, 24

Jones, Frances, 176

Jones, Noble, 174

Jordon, Lee, 142

Joyner, Charles, 4

Joyner, Robert L., 37

Kiawah, Cassique of. *See* Shadee
Kiawah Island, 85–91
Kiawah Resort Associates, 90
Kilgore, Jack L., 146
King, Martin Luther, Jr., 135
Knox, Rich, 29, 30
Kuwait Investment Company, 90
Kuwaiti government, 90

LaBruce, Flora McDonald, 11
LaBruce-Lemon House, 18
Lachicotte, Cap'n, 19
Ladson, Augustus, 80
Lady's Island, 124–28
Lafayette, Marquis de, 22, 23, 109
LaRoche Plantation, 105
Laurel Spring Plantation, 99
Lawrence, J. E., 168
Lawrence, Joseph H., 45
Lawrence, Mike, 73
Lee, Robert E., 115
Lee, William States, 117
Legare, Mrs. Francis Y., Sr., 70, 71
Lemon Island, 130
LeMoyne, Jacque, 149
Liberty Lodge, 18
Lincoln, Abraham, 55
Lipton company, 79
Lishman, Bill, 33
Little Edisto Plantation, 105
Little Goat Island, 44
London (Yonges Island). *See* Willtown
Long Island. *See* Isle of Palms

Long, J. C., 46
Look-out Island. *See* Pinckney Island
Loomis, Alfred, 166, 167, 168
Lords of Discipline, The, 177
Lords Proprietors, 38, 49, 80, 85, 86
Lowndes, Amarinthia, 93

Mackey, Alexander, 155
Mackey Island. *See* Pinckney Island
Maggie (ghost), 175
Maggioni, L. P., 100
Magnolia Garden Club, 76
Magwood family, 40
Manigault, Elizabeth, 93
Manigault, Gabriel, 93
Manigault, William H., 95
Marguerite, 82
Marine Biological Laboratory, 60
Marshall, Alex, 82
Marshall, George, 52
"Marshall Reservation, the," 52
Marshlands, 60
Martin, Chlotilde, 99, 168
Martinangel, Mrs. Philip, 173, 174
Martinangel, Philip, 173, 174
Mary Dunn Cemetery, 173
Mary Field Elementary School, 176, 177
Maxwell, William Rivers, 35
Mayo, Bobby, 128
Mayo, Mrs. Oscar, 128
Mayo, Oscar, 128
McAllister, Ward, 96
McLeod, M. L., 99, 123
McTeer, J. E., 138, 139

Mdivani, Alexis, 98
Medical College of South Carolina, 60, 78
Melrose Golf Club, 178
Melrose Plantation, 174, 178, 179
Michaux, André, 78, 79
Middleton, Henry, 156
Middleton Place Gardens, 78
Middleton, Sally, 156
Mikell, Isaac Jenkins, 104–7, 109, 114, 115, 123
Mikell, Isaac Jenkins, Jr., 107
Milton, 94
Misener Marine, 142
Mitchell, Sam, 124
Mongin, David, 180
Mongin, John, 173
Mongin River, 172
Monroe, John, 174
Moore's Landing, 43
Morgan Island, 130
Morris, Ann, 93
Morris Island, 66–68
Morris, Lewis, 93, 94
Mosquito Creek, 28
Moultrie, William, 50, 51
Mount Carmel Church, 177
Mount Pleasant Plantation, 32, 33
Muddy Creek Plantation, 160
Mulberry Grove Plantation, 3
Murray, Chalmers S., 113
Murray, Ellen, 134
Murrells Inlet, 7
Myrtle Beach, 43

Napoleon, 132
Nesbit-Noburn House, 18
New London. *See* Willtown
New River, 172
New, Robert, 67
New Towne, 59, 60
Nicklaus, Jack, 178
Normie, 64
North Beach Lighthouse, 142
North Carolina Hunting Club, 166
North Edisto River, 82, 114
North Inlet, 26
North Island, 21–29, 33, 34, 37
North Island Lighthouse, 24
North Santee Bay, 28
North Santee River, 28, 29

Oak Island, 109
Oakhurst Plantation, 96
Oaklodge, 93
Ocean Course, 170
Old Seabrook Mansion, 108, 109, 115, 116, 123
Old White Church, 132
Ordinance of Secession, 108, 114
Original Dixieland Swing Band, 66
Osceola, 52
O'Sullivan, Florentia, 49

Pacific Guano Company, 129
Pacific Island. *See* Chisolm Island
Paquin, Anna, 33
Parker, Peter, 50, 51
Parris, Alexander, 150

Parris Island, 148–53
Pawley, George, 14
Pawley House, 13, 18
Pawley, Percival, 13, 14
Pawleys Island, 13–20
Pee Dee River, 35
Pelican Inn, 16, 18
Penn Center, 135
Penn School, 134, 135
Peter's Point, 105–7, 109, 115, 123
Philbrick, Edward, 135
Phoenix, 59
Pinckney, Charles, 155
Pinckney, Charles Cotesworth, 155, 156, 158
Pinckney, Eliza Lucas, 155
Pinckney Island, 154–58
Pinckney Island National Wildlife Refuge, 158
Pine Island, 44
Pinehurst Tea Farm, 79
"Place of Blood," 173
"plat-eye," 112
Pocohontas, 164
Poe, Edgar Allen, 51, 52
Polwanna Island, 130
Pope, Squire, 174
Porgy, 64, 65
Porgy and Bess, 64, 65, 89
Port Royal, 148, 150, 160, 164
Port Royal Experiment, 134
Port Royal Plantation, 171
President's Stand, the, 25
Prevost, Augustine, 73
Prince George Winyah Church, 14

Prince of Tides, The, 177
Pringle, Elizabeth Allston, 16
Prioleau, Julia M., 146
Pritchard Island, 141
Prospect Hill Plantation, 94–96, 99, 100, 101
Proteus, 67
Pulaski, Casimir, 146
Punta de Santa Elena. *See* St. Helena Island

Quexos, Pedro de, 159, 170

Rabbit Point Plantation, 105
Raccoon Key, 41
Rainey, Roy L., 166
Ramshorn Creek, 172
Raynor, George, 87
red wolf breeding program, 42, 43
Renty, 15
Revolutionary War, 22, 39, 50, 73, 87, 108, 146, 156, 173
Rhett, William, 49
Ribaut, Jean, 148, 150
Richardson, Mary Roper, 76, 77
Riding Committee, 62
Rising Sun, 69
Rivers, E. L., 63
"Rocks, The," 80
Rockville, 81–83, 86
Rockville Races, 81
Rogel, Father, 102
Rouffi, Guillaume, 149
Royal, C. C., 89, 90
Royal, Eugenia Mae, 90

Ruby, 67
Ruffra, Joseph, 96
Rumbling of the Chariot Wheels, 107
Rutledge, Archibald, 40

Sampit River, 35
Sams, B. B., 81
Samuel, Robert, 118
"Sand Crabs," 49
Sandford, Robert, 49, 79, 80, 85, 86, 87
Sandy Cot, 18
Santa Elena's Day, 131
Santee Indians, 34
Sasaki, Hideo, 170
Savannah, 142
Screven, John, 2, 160
Sea Cloud, 123
Sea Island Regatta, 83
Sea Pines Plantation, 161, 170
Seabrook, Carolina de Lafayette. *See* Hopkinson, Carolina de Lafayette Seabrook
Seabrook family, 109, 123
Seabrook, George, Jr., 121
Seabrook Island, 68
Seabrook, J. Mason, 104
Seabrook, Whitmarsh Benjamin, 109
Seabrook, William, 108–10
sea-island cotton, 2–6, 62, 104, 109, 131
Seaside Plantation, 105, 118
Seewee Bay, 43
Seewee Indians, 38
Seminole Indians, 52

Shadee, 86
Shaftesbury, Earl of, 103
Shepherd, Charles, 78
Sherman, William T., 115, 117, 165, 174
Shuffeldt, R. W., 67
Shutes Folly Island, 55
Simons, Albert, 150
Singleton, Cato, 10, 11
Skull Creek, 154
Sladen, William, 33
Smalls, Sammy, 64
Smith, Prince, 80
Solomon Legare Island, 59. *See also* James Island
South Carolina Wildlife Department, 26–27, 32, 60
South Edisto River, 100, 102, 106
South Island, 21, 25, 26, 28–34, 36, 37
South Island Plantation, 30
Spanish Wells, 159. *See also* Hilton Head Island
Spanish Wells Plantation, 160
Speaker, Tris, 26
Spring Island, 130
Squash, 89
St. Helena Episcopal Church, 132
St. Helena Island, 129–39, 144, 151
St. Helena Parish, 132, 133
St. Helena Sound, 106, 115, 131
St. James A.M.E. Church, 35, 36
St. John's Colleton Parish, 80
St. Johns Episcopal Church, 75
St. Luke's Parish, 2

St. Paul's Parish, 2
St. Phillip Island, 141
St. Pierre Creek, 106, 110, 116
Stanyarne, John, 87
Starrow, Elise. *See* Yawkey, Elise
    Starrow
Stead, Mary, 156, 157
"Steeple Chase," 45
Steuben, 22
Stoddard, John, 174
Stoney, Jack, 161
Stoney, Maulsey, 112
Stono, Archibald, 69, 93
Stono Creek, 59, 60
Stono Ferry, 72, 73
Stono River, 72, 73, 84, 87
Strachan family, 178
Strachan Mansion, 178
sturgeon, 19
Sullivan's Island, 48–50, 52, 53, 54,
    93
Sully, Thomas, 5
Summer Academy, 18
Sumter, Thomas, 54
Swinton, Thomas L., 126

Talbot, John, 160
Teach, Edward, 145
Thorne, Landon K., 166, 167, 168
Tibwin Plantation, 38
Tidalholm, 132, 136
Tom Yawkey Wildlife Center, 21, 27,
    33, 37
Tombee, 131, 132
Towne, Laura, 134

Townsend, Hephzibah Jenkins, 110
Townsend, John F., 104
Trapier, Paul, 24
Trinity Episcopal Church, 111
Tucker, Thomas, 80

Union Baptist Church, 174, 176
United States Fish and Wildlife Ser-
    vice, 40
United States Marines, 150–52

Van der Horst family, 87, 88
Van der Horst, John, 87
Vanderhorst, Arnoldus, 87, 89
Vanderhorst, Elizabeth Raven, 87
Vanderhorst Mansion, 88
Villafane, Angel de, 131

Waccamaw Indians, 34
Waccamaw Neck, 14
Waccamaw River, 35
Wadmalaw Island, 78–84, 86
Wadmalaw Sound, 100
Waight, Abraham, 75
Wallace, Oliver T., 66
Wappoo Cut, 73
Washington, George, 51, 87, 156,
    157
Watts, Harry Dorsey, 31
Way, Charles S., Jr., 90
Webb, T. Ladsen, 84
Weldon, Felix de, 152
Weston, Elizabeth, 11
Weston, Pauline, 11
Weston, Plowden, 16

Whaley Plantation, 116

White Marsh Plantation, 35

Whitney, Eli, 3, 116

Wild Dunes Resort, 47

William I, 92

Willtown, 92, 93

Willtown Bluff, 93, 94, 95

Wiltown. *See* Willtown

Winyah Bay, 21, 23, 28

Withers family, 23, 24

Withers, Francis, 23

Withers, James, 23

Withers, John, 23

Withers, Richard, 23

Withers, Robert Francis, 23, 24

Withers, William, 23

Woodlawn Plantation, 124

Woolworth, Edna, 98

World War II, 40, 52, 53, 137, 169, 175

Wright, Abraham, 111

Wright, Elliott, 46

Yawkey, Elise Starrow, 30, 31

Yawkey Foundation, 32

Yawkey, Jean Hollander Hiller, 31, 32, 36

Yawkey, Thomas A., 26, 28, 30, 31, 36

Yawkey, William, 25, 26, 30–31, 35, 36

Yemassee Indians, 92, 173

Yonges Island, 92–101

Young, Arthur, 82

"Zebra Room, the," 97

Zion Chapel of Ease, 162